SCIENCE AND ENGINEERING PROGRAMS

On Target for Women?

Marsha Lakes Matyas
and
Linda Skidmore Dix,
editors

Ad hoc Panel on Interventions

Committee on Women in Science and Engineering

Office of Scientific and Engineering Personnel

National Research Council

NATIONAL ACADEMY PRESS
Washington, D.C. 1992

NOTICE: The project that is the subject of this report was approved by the Governing Board of the National Research Council, whose members are drawn from the councils of the National Academy of Sciences, the National Academy of Engineering, and the Institute of Medicine. This report has been reviewed by persons other than the authors according to procedures approved by a Report Review Committee consisting of members of the National Academy of Sciences, the National Academy of Engineering, and the Institute of Medicine.

The National Academy of Sciences is a private, nonprofit, self-perpetuating society of distinguished scholars engaged in scientific and engineering research, dedicated to the furtherance of science and technology and to their use for the general welfare. Upon the authority of the charter granted to it by the Congress in 1963, the Academy has a mandate that requires it to advise the federal government on scientific and technical matters. Dr. Frank Press is president of the National Academy of Sciences.

The National Academy of Engineering was established in 1964, under the charter of the National Academy of Sciences, as a parallel organization of outstanding engineers. It is autonomous in its administration and in the selection of its members, sharing with the National Academy of Sciences the responsibility for advising the federal government. The National Academy of Engineering also sponsors engineering programs aimed at meeting national needs, encourages education and research, and recognizes the superior achievements of engineers. Dr. Robert M. White is president of the National Academy of Engineering.

The Institute of Medicine was established in 1970 by the National Academy of Sciences to secure the services of eminent members of appropriate professions in the examination of policy matters pertaining to the health of the public. The Institute acts under the responsibility given to the National Academy of Sciences by its congressional charter to be an adviser to the federal government and, upon its own initiative, to identify issues of medical care, research, and education. Dr. Kenneth Shine is president of the Institute of Medicine.

The National Research Council was organized by the National Academy of Sciences in 1916 to associate the broad community of science and technology with the Academy's purposes of furthering knowledge and advising the federal government. Functioning in accordance with general policies determined by the Academy, the Council has become the principal operating agency of both the National Academy of Sciences and the National Academy of Engineering in providing services to the government, the public, and the scientific and engineering communities. The Council is administered jointly by both Academies and the Institute of Medicine. Dr. Frank Press and Dr. Robert M. White are chairman and vice chairman, respectively, of the National Research Council.

This material is based on work supported by the National Academy of Engineering's Technology Agenda to Meet the Competitive Challenge Program.

Library of Congress Catalog Card No. 92-61248
International Standard Book Number 0-309-04778-1

Additional copies of this report are available from:
National Academy Press
2101 Constitution Avenue, NW
Washington, DC 20418

S-617
Printed in the United States of America

iii

OFFICE OF SCIENTIFIC AND ENGINEERING PERSONNEL

ADVISORY COMMITTEE ON STUDIES AND ANALYSES

ACKNOWLEDGMENTS

The Committee on Women in Science and Engineering (CWSE) is a continuing committee within the National Research Council's Office of Scientific and Engineering Personnel. The goal of the Committee is to increase the participation of women in science and engineering by convening meetings, conducting research, and disseminating data about the status of women in these fields. The Committee's core activities are funded by a consortium of federal and private organizations. For their roles in securing contributions of partial funding for the core activities of the Committee, their sharing with the Committee the concerns of their organizations relevant to the Committee's mandate, and their participation in the Committee's deliberations about topics that it might examine in order to address the underparticipation of women in science and engineering, we are grateful to the following sponsor representatives: Bruce Guile, National Academy of Engineering; Harriet Zuckerman, Andrew W. Mellon Foundation; Charles R. Bowen, International Business Machines Corporation; Mark Myers, Xerox Corporation; Burton H. Colvin, National Institute for Standards and Technology; Marguerite Hays, Department of Veterans Affairs; Margrete S. Klein, National Science Foundation (NSF); Sherri McGee, National Aeronautics and Space Administration (NASA); Sheila Rosenthal, U.S. Environmental Protection Agency; and Ruth Ann Verell, U.S. Department of Energy's (DOE) Office of Energy Research. In addition, we acknowledge the input of Richard Stephens, DOE, and Margaret Finarelli and Frank Owens, NASA, during the initial discussions about the roles of the Committee and federal agencies in increasing the participation of women in science and engineering. Finally, we recognize the financial support given by the Alfred P. Sloan Foundation, through the direction of program officer Harry Weiner, specifically for the holding of the Conference on Science and Engineering Programs.

The Committee is pleased to include within the various chapters of this report information conveyed by individuals knowledgeable of the issues and strategies for addressing them: Linda S. Wilson, Elizabeth Stage, Marsha Lakes Matyas, Joan Sherry, Garrison Sposito, Esther M. Conwell, Linda Skidmore Dix, and Mildred S. Dresselhaus. These authors relied not only on their own knowledge of the issues, but also on the presentations of several experts who are listed in Appendix B of this report.

The Committee is indebted to several staff of the National Research Council's Office of Scientific and Engineering Personnel. Alan Fechter, executive director, offered valuable advice during the planning of the conference. Pamela Ebert Flattau, director of studies and surveys, helped to structure both the conference agenda and the format of this report. Gaelyn Davidson, project assistant for CWSE, handled conference logistics and all word processing for this report. Assisting with the development of graphics was Valerie Andrewlevich, senior secretary. Throughout this project—from initial planning of the conference through dissemination of this report—activities have been coordinated by the CWSE study director, Linda Skidmore Dix.

Finally, we acknowledge the special efforts of three individuals: Marsha Lakes Matyas and Linda Skidmore Dix, who devoted much time editing the manuscripts during the first six months of 1992, and Mildred S. Dresselhaus, CWSE chair whose oversight for this work led her to carry the manuscript halfway around the world. The Committee appreciates their efforts to compile information from a variety of sources that would present an overview of the current knowledge about postsecondary S&E interventions in place on university campuses and in the work setting.

FOREWORD

The fraction of working women participating in the scientific and engineering work force is smaller than that of men. However, as the need for scientists and engineers increases for the U.S. R&D enterprise, women should find greater opportunities to pursue careers in these fields. Nonetheless, to increase women's participation in science and engineering, many barriers must be overcome.

The National Research Council's Committee on Women in Science and Engineering (CWSE) has several important roles related to these challenges. One of these roles is to inform both the science and engineering community and the public of the need to increase the participation of women in scientific and engineering careers—to increase not only economic competitiveness but also educational and occupational equity. Another is to collect and disseminate information on programs designed to address that need. To meet these mandates, in November 1991 the Committee held a Conference on Science and Engineering Programs, with three objectives:

1   To examine a sample of interventions from the wide spectrum known to have been established in the private and public sectors with the objective of increasing the participation of U.S. citizens, both men and women, in science and engineering careers;

2   To determine the characteristics shared by programs considered to meet that objective; and

3   To discuss methods of implementing such programs on a broader scale.

The conference was an important activity of the Committee in several ways. First, it brought together both initiators and administrators of interventions, as well as funders of those that have seemed effective—as measured by whether participants actually completed science or engineering (S&E) degrees or obtained employment in an S&E field. Second, it introduced those newly interested in the issue of women's underparticipation in science and engineering to those who have been working to address this situation for some time. Finally, it heightened awareness of what universities, corporations, foundations, and other groups are doing to increase the quantity and quality of U.S. students pursuing careers in the sciences and engineering.

The result of the conference is this report, which summarizes presentations by many experts in this area and presents information on specific strategies for increasing the participation of women in science and engineering—at the undergraduate and graduate levels of study and in all employment sectors. This document also incorporates the more informal deliberations at the conference.

This report is unusual in that its chapters were authored by individuals, not by the Committee on Women in Science and Engineering (CWSE). While the views expressed here do not necessarily reflect those of the National Research Council, its Office of Scientific and Engineering Personnel (OSEP), or CWSE, the Committee believes that the chapters accurately reflect discussions at the Committee-sponsored conference. The report has benefitted in its writing from the experience and expertise of the chapter authors.

Those expected to benefit from the contents of this document include the broad community of policy makers, educators, employers, researchers, and scientists and engineers themselves. Specifically, it is envisioned that members of the following groups will find the information contained herein useful: women S&E undergraduate and graduate students; women scientists and engineers employed in academe, companies, and federal agencies; undergraduate and graduate deans; and CEOs/VPs for human resources in U.S. companies.

The Committee hopes that both conference participants and those unable to participate in the conference will find the report helpful as they work to increase the quantity and improve the quality of U.S. students, particularly women and members of racial/ethnic minority groups, pursuing careers in science and engineering.

Linda S. Wilson
Chair
Office of Scientific and Engineering
Personnel

PREFACE

From its initial meeting in 1991, the National Research Council's Committee on Women in Science and Engineering (CWSE) has expressed concern about the decreasing numbers (and percentages) of U.S. citizens receiving degrees at all levels in science and engineering. Data from the surveys of incoming college and university freshmen conducted by the Higher Education Research Institute and from the National Science Foundation's Surveys of Science, Social Science, and Engineering Graduates indicated that increasing numbers of U.S. students initially expressing interest in science and engineering (S&E) careers switch out of S&E study as undergraduates or after having obtained baccalaureates in science or engineering. This phenomenon of "field switching" led the Committee, in turn, to take an interest in the "supply and demand issue," namely whether the supply of U.S.-citizen scientists and engineers would be sufficient to meet the demands for highly skilled personnel posed by U.S. companies, educational institutions, and the government. While the "supply and demand issue" is open to debate, the Committee believes that changing U.S. demography serves to intensify the debate.

Traditionally, scientists and engineers in the United States have been white males; and we know that, during the next decade in particular, the percentage of white males reflected in the net new entrants to the work force will be decidedly smaller than in the past. Thus, there is an important opportunity to meet the nation's needs for scientists and engineers by increasing the numbers of women and minorities receiving advanced preparation in those fields.

When considering the many possible topics for its first conference, CWSE identified a significant gap in our knowledge concerning the utilization of interventions for women in science and engineering: although much research has been conducted on these interventions, the knowledge gained from those programs has never been consolidated to give a clear picture of what strategies are effective, particularly at the postsecondary and employment levels. The Committee determined, therefore, that an examination of postsecondary programs designed to recruit and retain U.S. citizens in science and engineering was warranted and decided to focus on those targeted to women.

Prior to holding the conference, "Science and Engineering Programs: On Target for Women?," Committee staff canvassed various organizations to determine the nature and range of interventions and relied on a variety of sources to gather information about them. Individuals, notified of the Committee's interest in S&E interventions and plans to sponsor a conference on this topic, were asked to provide basic information about specific program(s) with which they were familiar. Those responding to the Committee's request for information, as well as others in the research and funding communities, were asked to share, at the conference, information regarding the spectrum of postsecondary programs supported by the federal government and the private sector, components of successful recruitment and retention programs, and models for programs that might be adopted by other organizations. Because of widespread evidence about national involvement in programs at the precollege level, the Committee decided to make the subject of the conference "postsecondary programs." Programs highlighted at the conference were selected in terms of their effectiveness in meeting program objectives, as reported by groups such as the White House Task Force on Women, Minorities, and the Handicapped and the American Association for the Advancement of Science.

This report, a combination of authored papers and distillation of the issues discussed at the conference, has been designed to (1) heighten public awareness of activities that address the underutilization of a major component of this country's S&E talent pool and (2) disseminate information to those interested in achieving increased participation of women in S&E careers, particularly people who want to implement interventions but have limited funds to do so. This report has two major features: (1) descriptions of the components of effective postsecondary programs at each education level and in each employment sector and (2) a listing of effective programs whose administrators are willing to serve as resources for those wishing to establish interventions at their institutions or to upgrade programs already in operation.

The plenary presentations by Linda Wilson and Elizabeth Stage at the conference (see Chapters 1 and 2) set the tone for both the conference and this report: to establish goals for the scientific and engineering community; to take a careful look at those strategies that work; to approach the topic of interventions as a research problem with defined theories, where programs and theories need to be subjected to thorough evaluation; and to maximize the resources available for interventions by establishing extensive and effective communications networks among all those involved. In Chapter 3, Marsha

Lakes Matyas presents data that assess the current status of women in post-secondary levels of S&E education and employment. The subsequent panels, formal and informal discussions, and conversations-in-the-hall during the conference yielded a wealth of information. Chapters 4-8 summarize much of this information and convey the conclusions and recommendations made by the conference participants. Each of the individually authored chapters presents information on specific programs designed to improve the current situation for women in science and engineering. Each chapter then concludes with suggestions for future initiatives in addressing the underparticipation of women in careers in the sciences and engineering. Those suggestions, summarized below, do not reflect an in-depth examination of S&E interventions by the Committee on Women in Science and Engineering but, rather, the belief of the Committee that these suggestions are representative of those made by participants at the Committee-sponsored conference.

Undergraduate Initiatives

The conference discussions and a number of recent reports recommend initiatives for increasing the participation of women in science and engineering at the undergraduate level:

- Higher education institutions should monitor student progress to assess where "losses" of S&E students, especially women and minorities, occur.
- Specific funding sources should be targeted at women.
- Comprehensive interventions should be targeted toward women and implemented in diverse institutions.
- The research base on interventions for women in science and engineering at the undergraduate level should be expanded by funding longitudinal evaluations of selected programs.
- New models should be developed, evaluated, revised, and disseminated for involving faculty members in strategies to increase the participation of undergraduate women in science and engineering.

Graduate and Postdoctoral Initiatives

Future directions for interventions in the graduate education of women in science and engineering are suggested in Chapter 5:

- "Confidence building" techniques should be developed so that women graduate students gain both scientific expertise and effective communication skills that will permit them to go forward in careers in science and mathematics with a high degree of comfort and confidence.
- To retain graduate students in the sciences and engineering, departments and institutions must develop programs of positive incentives for faculty.
- The "level playing field" concept for women graduate students must be articulately and concretely demonstrated by upper management of the academic institution.
- At all levels—institution, department, and individual mentor— sensitivity, flexibility, and understanding of child bearing/rearing issues must be demonstrated to avoid discouragement and loss of talented female graduate students from these fields into others where time for a family is more easily managed.
- Resolving issues related to balancing family and scientific career goals for women graduate students must be a high priority for any academic institution.

Interventions To Recruit and Retain
Women Science and Engineering Faculty

Given the paucity of major interventions to promote the careers of women scientists and engineers in academe, the Irvine conference discussion focused on strategies to develop such programs. Following are four broad strategies that Garrison Sposito proposes in Chapter 6 for implementation by universities:

- Establish an Office on the Status of Women Faculty Members, whose director is a senior female professor with line responsibility to the chief administrative officer of the campus.
- Revise the tenure process on campus to ensure that untenured women faculty members are indeed reviewed by their peers during the probationary period and that every tenure-review committee has at least one female member.
- Create a family-friendly workplace environment by establishing flexible work schedules, job sharing, and subsidized, proximate child care as *standard* features of campus programs for the faculty.

- Allow maximum flexibility in working conditions consistent with carrying out responsibilities of teaching and research.

Interventions To Recruit and Retain
Women Scientists and Engineers in Industry

To achieve women's participation in industrial employment comparable to that in the academic and government sectors requires a directed program of strategic and sustained activities developed jointly by women scientists and engineers and the companies for which they work:

- Women should be given incentives to seek employment in industry in greater numbers than at present.
- Women should band together within companies in order to improve skills and performance levels throughout their group, and to overcome some of the built-in organizational barriers to learning and promotion.
- Companies should allow maximum flexibility in working conditions consistent with getting the job done well.
- To increase the number of women gaining industrial employment in science and engineering, companies should expand the universe from which they recruit entry-level employees.

Interventions of the Federal Government
To Recruit and Retain Women Scientists and Engineers

The National Research Council's Committee on Scientists and Engineers in the Federal Government examined recruitment, retention, and utilization issues and noted two that require further research: "what can be done to enhance federal recruitment of scientists and engineers, especially women and minorities at the entry level, and retention of all scientists and engineers at the midcareer level," and "what institutional decision-making process should be altered and in what way."* Specifically,

---

*Alan K. Campbell and Linda S. Dix (eds.), *Recruitment, Retention, and Utilization of Federal Scientists and Engineers* (Washington, DC: National Academy Press, 1990).

- The federal government and individual agencies should assess what else can be done and develop interventions for both women and men.
- The federal government should consider programs targeting women S&E employees, similar to those existing in the private sector. In particular, the "glass-cutter" program designed by conference participants would be an appropriate starting point for federal agencies to address the issue of increasing their employment of women scientists and engineers.

The particular goals of the Conference on Science and Engineering Programs were to review some programs deemed effective because of their ability to assist program participants in achieving degrees in science and engineering and to try to determine what elements of those programs enhance both education and careers in science and engineering for women. Throughout the conference, consideration was given to how to make best use of human resources and financial resources to widen the pipeline in a constructive way with a long-term impact. Some actions necessary for establishing and maintaining S&E intervention are discussed in the last chapter of this report.

Finally, the material in the appendixes may be particularly useful to those interested in establishing contact with administrators for a variety of S&E programs at the postsecondary level. In Appendix A one may find key information about a variety of programs; the reader is cautioned, however, that these tables provide information about a representative sample and are not inclusive of all programs targeted to potential scientists and engineers.

The Committee on Women in Science and Engineering made no attempt to ascertain the effectiveness of current programs. In part, this decision was made in consideration of the fact that many interventions have not been evaluated to determine the extent to which programmatic goals have been achieved. Thus, one action that is recommended is the inclusion of an evaluation component within all S&E interventions in the future. This report provides the first step in developing the conceptual framework that is needed to conduct formal evaluative work.

Mildred S. Dresselhaus
Chair
Committee on Women
in Science and Engineering

CONTENTS

xvii

xviii

LIST OF FIGURES

SCIENCE AND ENGINEERING
PROGRAMS

THE BENEFITS OF DIVERSITY IN THE SCIENCE AND ENGINEERING WORK FORCE

Linda S. Wilson

Linda Wilson, chair of the National Research Council's Office of Scientific and Engineering Personnel and president of Radcliffe College, has made important contributions to the position of women not only in science and engineering, but in scholarly activities in general. Before going to Radcliffe College, Wilson was Vice President for Research at the University of Michigan.

A graduate of Newcomb College, Tulane University, she earned a Ph.D. in inorganic chemistry at the University of Wisconsin. She went on to teach and conduct research at the University of Maryland, then pursued a second career devoted to fostering and oversight of research and graduate education. She served in senior administrative posts at Washington University, the University of Illinois, and the University of Michigan. Dr. Wilson has long been active in the national science policy arena, where she has contributed to strengthening the relationships among universities, the government, and industry. Her publications span the fields of chemistry, science policy, and higher education.

In 1959, the President's Science Advisory Committee issued a major statement on Education for the Age of Science. That statement began with the premises of the American system of education. It spoke to the varieties of talents in our population and recognized the need for continuing adjustment to keep pace with the problems and opportunities that would face our country in the coming ages. Two of the several premises that were expressed in 1959 were that:

(1)   "No child shall be deprived of the fullest opportunity to develop his talents" and

(2)   "No one shall be condemned to a lowly position or elevated to a high one by the mere circumstance of the wealth, power, and prestige of his ancestors."

The committee's statement explicitly addressed, albeit very briefly, the changing role of women in society—as a result of modern technology, which provided a release from domestic drudgery and, as a result of earlier marriage, which advanced the time at which women could make substantial commitments outside the home. The committee at that time concluded that "women constitute an enormous potential resource for research, scholarship, and teaching" and called for "conscious efforts to assist women to make the contributions of which they are capable."

As I read that now, through the lens of 1991, I note the presumption that married women should stay home, and I note the reference to those contributions "of which they are capable" and wonder exactly what the committee meant. Expectations are broader now. Since 1959, we have come a very long way in developing talent generally and in developing science and engineering talent specifically. We have also made strong progress in educating more of our population, especially women. Now, in 1991, it is nevertheless sobering to look back at the aspirations that were expressed at that time and to realize how much those ideals have been imperfectly executed. The task of tapping fully the potential of the talents of our population is far from complete. Indeed, in some ways we seem to be losing ground. Furthermore, for various reasons, the stakes are higher now and the urgency is much more acute.

Our progress has been seriously slowed by a number of factors but perhaps by none as inhibiting as the cultural beliefs and traditions that have circumscribed the expectations that we have for the roles and contributions of a substantial part of our population, namely women and minorities. Biases regarding gender, race, ethnicity, and class have interfered with our pursuit of our expressed ideals. Although we are a nation of immigrants, we have learned very imperfectly how to understand, how to value, and how to benefit from our differences.

Now, as we approach a new century and take a new look, we must renew our efforts to develop our human resources to their full potential and to engage that rich array of talent in the pursuit of larger common purposes, to pursue a better life for all of the people in this nation and in the world. Recruitment and retention of talent in the sciences and engineering are an important part of the larger challenge of broad and full development of human potential. Our society has high requirements for talent and creativity

2

in these fields. Our efforts to find and develop them will have valuable spin-off for other fields as well.

I will focus my remarks on the more specific challenges with regard to women and minorities, and especially to those facing women. I would like to contribute the compelling arguments for assuring full participation of women and minorities in our society and particularly in science and engineering; the full meaning of the term "access;" a framework for discussing and evaluating interventions to enhance access and achievement; and the identification of some fundamental issues that will be important to the pursuit of our goals.

The Compelling Arguments

There are four compelling arguments for opening the doors, removing the barriers, and encouraging and enabling the full participation of women and minorities. These arguments are valid for participation in all aspects of our society, but perhaps are especially so in science and engineering.

First, there is the simple argument for equitable treatment of all of our citizens, an argument which should stand on its own and be totally sufficient, an argument that emerged as part of the civil rights and human rights movements of the mid-century and which had its roots in many of the movements that had taken place before. Some of the most critical legislation was based on this argument alone. Substantial progress has, in fact, been made in changing the rules that previously barred women and minorities from entry and participation—in education, in the workplace, and in social environments.

The second argument—the economic argument—has gained increasing attention as our nation has become increasingly dismayed by its waning leadership in the international economic arena. The nature of the economic base of this country presents a growing need for skilled workers, for knowledge workers, for intellectual talent, and for ingenuity. Since the new entrants to the work force by the year 2000 will be predominantly women and minorities, our economic security will depend on how well we have educated, trained, and incorporated these individuals into full participation.

In addition to these two very powerful arguments of equity and

3

economics, a persuasive third argument can be made. Women and minorities, as new entrants to the work force, represent an important source of renewal. New entrants bring questions, fresh ideas, new and different perspectives on old problems, new energies, and new skills. They are not blinded by the familiar. The experience they bring enlarges the repertoire of strategies that can be employed. They are therefore an important factor in making successful transitions and for accommodating change. Our country faces enormous transitions, for it is quite clear that business as usual is not the name of the game. The full participation of women and minorities contributes a diversity in the citizenry and in the work force, and that gives our society added resilience and adaptability—just what we need to accomplish and to guide rapid change. The strategy of using diversity to assure long-term vitality is not new, of course. It has worked very well in nature, in investments, in business development, in education, and in our culture.

Finally, a fourth argument can be made for women and minorities' full participation in society, especially in science and engineering fields: the "public will argument." Many of the challenges we now face will not yield just to knowledge and innovation. Progress on them will require a concerted public will—a broad and sustained commitment to make short-term sacrifices where necessary for long-term gain—as in the development of viable policies for energy, for education, for health care, and for the environment. In these areas especially, broad, decentralized activity is needed. These problems will not yield to tentative, intermittent effort. Nor will they be solved just by rules or proclamations issued by a remote elite. Without widespread and informed commitment to common purpose, solutions that involve disruption of expectations or impose economic or social discomfort will not be accepted. And even if they were to win initial acceptance, they would not be sustained. We need to *develop,* now more than ever, an informed, scientifically literate citizenry. We need to *engage* in serious attention on these issues in a substantive way, and we need to *sustain* our efforts for the long term. We cannot succeed on many critically important policy matters without the full participation of women and minorities, in both the development and the support of effective policy and action.

The Full Meaning of "Access"

Consider what is involved to gain women's full participation: full

4

access goes far beyond just opening the doors of educational institutions and the workplace. It means:

- changing and enlarging the expectations of students, teachers, supervisors, leaders, and the public in general about the capabilities and contributions of women;
- developing in women strong self-esteem and sense of self-competency—and discovering what experiences reinforce these attributes;
- reexamining assumptions that research accomplished using only male subjects yields valid conclusions for both males and females;
- recognizing and valuing the accomplishments of women so that both men and women have a better sense of their heritage and potential;
- seeking and exploring new perspectives on the fields of knowledge as new entrants bring new questions and different experiences to bear on discovery;
- identifying and understanding the barriers to women's progress in academic and professional careers so that these can be removed or overcome;
- addressing the communication challenges women and men face together in the classroom, in the home, in the workplace, and in volunteer activities so that they can be more effective partners in their endeavors; and
- acknowledging the underlying issues that threaten families, institutions, and communities so that creative and effective social policies can be developed and sustained.

Marilyn Heins, M.D., F.A.A.P., in her acceptance remarks when she was honored as a distinguished alumna of Radcliffe College, made an astute observation about national policies and full access for women. She pointed out that the workplaces in this country, unlike those of other industrial nations, are still governed by some policies, dating from the 1950s, which assumed that mothers stayed at home. Now, in the last decade of the century, two-thirds of mothers are in the work force. Dr. Heins asks, "Why have our policies not kept pace with the greatest societal change most of us will ever witness—the exponential and continuing rise of mothers employed outside the home?" The tension over this issue reflects opposing ideologies and paralysis with regard to child-care policies and facilities. **"We are the only**

5

industrialized nation in the world that pretends women are not in the work force." This paralysis, and the ideological tension that causes it, profoundly affect the nation's capacity to develop and utilize its human resources.

As we seek access for women in the fullest sense of the word, our effort and our accomplishments will enlarge opportunities for both men and women. They will enlarge opportunities for members of minority groups as well. We will learn more about teaching and learning; we will learn more about the interactions of individuals with institutions and social systems; and in the process, we will learn more about our institutions and systems themselves. With this knowledge we can make them better.

Frameworks for Discussing Interventions

Our pursuit of full access will involve the intervention strategies that you are here to describe and discuss today. There are several frameworks that one could use for guiding and organizing this discussion of interventions. The framework that has been chosen for the conference—the stages of education and the employment sectors—is especially useful for the intended broad audience of the results of your discussion. Within that framework, however, I suggest that it would be useful to categorize these interventions further, according to their principal focus or purpose. Are you addressing *systemic* change by your intervention, *organizational* change, or *personal change?*

Beyond these broad categories, interventions can be distinguished by the *nature* of the change involved. For example, if the intervention is focused at the organizational change level, does it address behavior or beliefs of employees or leaders, structure, or rules and working conditions? For an intervention at the personal level, will the focus be acquisition of skills or resources, change in relationships, enhancement of motivation, or improvement in sense of competence and well-being?

Still other questions might be considered regarding interventions:

●   What is the *degree of complexity* or multiplexity of the intervention? How probable is it that cause and effect relationships can be isolated for subsequent evaluation?

- What is the *duration* of the intervention? Is it continuous, periodic, or intermittent—or a single effort?
- What is the *degree of generalizability* or specificity of the intervention?

You will surely discover other useful categories as the result of the discussion of the conference. The search should be for the critical intervention strategies—those with the greatest leverage applied at the most critical junctures to effect lasting change. This is why categorization is important. We must design efficiency into this endeavor, for we do not have the luxury of a slow pace.

As you consider interventions, let me suggest another kind of framework, a framework for design of a specific intervention. First, there should be careful problem definition: focus on understanding what behavior or process needs modification, how that process works, and why it works the way it does. Next, one must fold in contextual changes and recognize that the planned interventions interface with other systems already in place, particularly the education system: consider subjective issues, identify and address the fears that will be raised by the proposed interventions, and consider some scenarios about how to handle the consequences and the interconnections. At that point, identify rather specifically what it is that you want to achieve. In fact, it is very important to revisit this particular question in a recurring way throughout one's planning, implementation, and evaluation. Yes, repeatedly concentrate attention on just what is it you are trying to achieve.

With those several considerations in mind, you should be ready to design the intervention and identify indicators of success. You need to be careful to distinguish qualitative and quantitative indicators, because not everything that is important is measurable. Not everything you design into your activity has to be measurable. There is the measurement and the monitoring of outcomes and the interpretation of those outcomes. You need to pay special attention to the feedback loops in this process. Finally, please, share the results: we must not continually reinvent every wheel.

Let me reiterate my encouragement to search very carefully for the important feedback loops in the interventions, to recognize and to come to grips with deeply-rooted beliefs and fears that will affect your success, to be scrupulous in distinguishing myth from reality, and to pay a great deal of attention to the changing external context for we are addressing a moving target as the social frontier advances.

As we plan and discuss the interventions to enhance the recruitment and retention of women in science and engineering, we must bear in mind that much of the design of the current work structures and environments were put in place a long time ago by people different from those who will work in them in the future. The design features of these organizational arrangements were influenced by another context, by previous problems, and by the operating styles of the leaders of that time. Indeed, a lot of our organizational structures were really shaped by their founder and first leader. Those organizational structures were designed without the benefit of our subsequent organizational, psychological, educational, sociological, and political science research. But even if that research had been done at the time the organizations were being designed, the results of that research might not have been brought to bear. The bridges between research, policy, and action were and are fragile: our organizational design activities have been and still are very much of a "try and try again" matter. Furthermore, much of the existing structure was based on anachronistic assumptions, assumptions that there would be a single wage-earner per family and that the wage-earner would be supported by a community network that was strong, by a school system that met basic needs of knowledge for the workplace, and by a family in which most of the home work would be done by those who stayed at home.

In reality, knowledge and information needs have far outstripped what our school systems provide. Our communities are unravelling and dispersing. Our families are being redefined. Dual wage-earners are now needed to support many traditional and redefined family groups in all but the most economically advantaged elite.

Also bear in mind that the cultural bases for the pattern of roles men and women play run very, very deep. They are linked to basic conceptualizations of masculinity and femininity. For 20 years the leading definition of masculinity provided by subjects of the Yankelovich Monitor survey, a large nationwide poll that has tracked social attitudes, has been "being a good provider for his family" (Faludi, 1991). The socialization that males have experienced in growing up aims toward that responsibility. It is out of that goal and the set of accompanying expectations that

8

competitiveness, beliefs about the workplace, and beliefs about women's having limited roles arise. Interventions that are insensitive to these basic conceptual roots will encounter difficult problems and may fail. But interventions that are sensitive to them give us the opportunity to develop a new understanding of the values of the diversity among men and women and to gain the benefit that diversity can provide.

Some Fundamental Issues

Four fundamental issues will affect our progress in achieving the goals.

1   **Do we intend for women (and minorities) to become full participants or just to remain as "guests"?**

If we intend their full participation, then the enterprise must change to be hospitable operationally and psychologically for both women and men and for minorities and the majority. I am convinced that changes to achieve that goal of full participation, full membership rather than just guest status, will increase the ease of recruitment and retention in science and engineering for both men and women.

We need to shift from a *singular* strategy of "survival of the fittest" to a *broader portfolio* of strategies to develop human potential to its fullest. Benjamin Bloom's studies reveal that talent and capability are far more widespread in the population than our educational systems and policies assume (Pearson et al., 1989). Bloom identified a number of key factors for encouraging and developing that widespread talent. He noted the importance not only of identifying the talent, but also of nurturing it and *of providing a sphere of action for it.* If you think about women and minorities, you discover that what has been largely unavailable to them is a sphere in which they can feel that they have a rightful, acknowledged place.

A recent editorial in the Boston Globe by Phyllis Goldfarb, professor of law at Boston College, addressed the Anita Hill-Clarence Thomas hearings. She spoke to the issue of women's silence, using the example of Anita Hill's reticence to file a formal grievance at the time of the incidents that triggered the hearings. Prof. Goldfarb pointed out that women's silence, for which Anita Hill was criticized, is extremely understandable if one examines it in terms of power relationships. She said, **"The powerful stand at the gatehouse of knowledge and language."** That is a profound insight, relevant for our

9

exploration of the environment for recruiting talent to science and engineering. In these fields, male perceptions of the world, male perspectives of how people function, and males' own socialization toward intense competitiveness and power have been a major part of what has shaped an environment that is now not very hospitable to the newcomers we seek to engage.

We cannot overlook that factor, but we have to be very careful not to "throw the baby out with the bath water." We are quite unlikely to succeed in any of our endeavors if we totally ignore and reject competition. What we need to do is to move on to a much more sophisticated plane and have a portfolio or repertoire of strategies that includes competition, complementarity, cooperation, and collaboration—each selectively used at its most effective juncture.

The interventions that you are exploring and designing can provide the cognitive and social bridges so that the number of women and minorities participating can increase to a critical mass. Once that critical mass is achieved, the environment will begin to change as their contributions help to shape what we do and how we do it.

2   **How can the cultural norms of the various science and engineering disciplines and professions be reconciled with our needs for recruiting and nurturing human potential?**

Within our fields of science and engineering, and also in other fields of knowledge, there are quite different cultural norms for the way work should proceed, what people should do, and how they think and interact. The existence of these various cultures, or folkways, may be a response to social and psychological differences among people, but I doubt that the differences in distribution of women and men among the various fields has any basis in inherent differences between men and women.

I suggest that we should be challenged, as we design our interventions, to look carefully at the cultures of each field and to make more explicit what the folkways of the fields are. Once they are more apparent, we can examine them to see whether the folkways represent core values to be preserved or habits and traditions that could be adjusted to make the fields more open to women and minorities and, at the same time, more productive for all.

10

3   How will the values that are now reflected by employers of scientists and engineers resonate with the values of the men and women who will work in their organizations?

Each year, in a national survey (Astin et al., 1990; Dey et al., 1991), we ask students about their values. Men and women often differ in the order, or hierarchy, of their values. Men are often more focused on career goals and on earning power. Women tend to put as a higher priority doing good, doing something for improving life and the human condition.

These hierarchies of values need to be recognized and understood as to their roots and the way they coincide or fail to coincide with the values prevalent in industry, particularly the defense industry, and in academe. We must think this through carefully so that we can understand their implications for our international interdependencies—our interdependencies scientifically, technologically, economically, environmentally, and in health.

4   What role will the media play in enhancing recruitment and development of talent in science and engineering?

At present the representation of women and scientists by the media, in advertising and in entertainment, is working at cross purposes with what we need to achieve. In the media, advertisements often demean, marginalize, and trivialize women. Scientists and engineers are often ridiculed. They may be cast as monsters or as evil. These representations of women and minorities and of scientists and engineers simply do not help.

Television is a powerful tool. It is potentially a very valuable educative force, but it is not now a positive factor in supporting our national objectives in human resource development. Super-sophisticated technical prowess claims the minds and attention of the viewers, but the technical virtuosity far outstrips the substantive value. Such powerful distractions from and competition to education are dysfunctional in a society that must increasingly be broadly literate. One result of the power of television is a marginalization of school education in the minds of students. The effect goes well beyond science, engineering, and math and represents lost opportunities of enormous proportions. It reflects a reordering of the values of our society, a reordering which I must believe is unintended and correctable. It can only be corrected, however, if we can effectively exert our public will. This is why it is so important for us to recognize the roles that women and men, majority and minority, play in developing the public will. We need the full participation of all.

Final Challenges

I would like to encourage you, and the Committee as it pursues its work, to consider the very special value of longitudinal studies for assessing and for understanding the change in human performance. To show you why I think that it is so important, I will refer to a fascinating report by Clifford Adelman on the recent study of the educational careers and labor market experience of men and women in the high school class of 1972 from the time they graduated from high school until they were 32 years old (Adelman, 1991). His report provides some important good news amidst the usual worries about the preparedness of our nation for effective participation in the global economy. He points out that:

> If we play it right, if we allow our oft-stated beliefs in rewards for educational achievement to govern, if economic justice can determine economic strategy, then the women of the United States will make the difference. We will not be eclipsed and our standard of living will not fall if we play it right and play it just, for our special asset as we enter the next century is that U.S. women of all races are the best educated and best trained in the world and will constitute 64 percent of the new entrants to the work force over the next 10 years. They comprise over half the enrollees and degree recipients at all levels of education except the doctorate and first professional levels and even there the gap should close by the end of the decade.

Furthermore, this longitudinal study of a very large sample of individuals over time revealed that *the women out-performed the men* on many different dimensions:

- academic performance in high school,
- receipt of awards for scholarships for postsecondary education,
- the rate of completion of college degrees (both bachelor's degrees and associate's degrees),

12

- academic performance in college in terms of grade-point average, averaged over all fields and also in statistics and calculus,
- change of educational aspirations by the end of college toward the pursuit of graduate degrees,
- rate of use of continuing education after the age of 30,
- the development of positive attitudes toward education,
- the belief that they truly benefitted from schooling,
- finding their education relevant to their work and working a great deal with ideas (the engine for an information economy), and
- positive attitude towards working conditions, relations on the job, and development of new skills.

Men and women performed about equally in terms of their SAT scores when they had studied two years' worth of math and science, and they performed about equally in their rate of continuation of education after high school. *Women scored lower than men* in three areas:

1   At the high school level, their educational aspirations and plans were lower than those of men, reflecting their socialization.
2   Women experienced more genuine unemployment than men.
3   Women were paid less than men, on the average.

In only 7 out of 33 occupations did women achieve pay equity with men, but what was especially noteworthy was that women who had earned 8 credits of college-level math did achieve pay equity with men.

These results emphasize for me the value of the longitudinal studies. We would not know about those very valuable assets that women provide in their performance and their attitudes had the same people not been followed over a long span of years. A longitudinal study provides a very much more detailed and accurate picture than do snapshot surveys from time to time. That is one of the reasons that the Office of Scientific and Engineering Personnel persists in several of the longitudinal studies that it conducts.

Finally, let me exhort you to recognize the importance of systematic, well-documented effort, the necessity for structural and systemic change, and the very great importance of encouraging and sharing with each other.

REFERENCES

Adelman, Clifford. 1991. *Women at Thirty Something*. Washington, DC: U.S. Department of Education.

Astin, Alexander W., William S. Korn, and Ellyne R. Berz. 1990. *The American Freshman: National Norms for Fall 1990*. Los Angeles: Cooperative Institutional Research Program, University of California; and American Council on Education.

Dey, Eric, Alexander W. Astin, and William S. Korn. 1991. *The American Freshman: Twenty-Five Year Trends*. Los Angeles: Cooperative Institutional Research Program, University of California; and American Council on Education.

Faludi, Susan. 1991. *Backlash: The Undeclared War Against American Women*. New York: Crown Publishers, Inc., p. 65.

Pearson, Carol S., Donna L. Shavlik, and Judith G. Touchton. 1989. *Educating the Majority: Women Challenge Tradition in Higher Education*. Washington, DC: American Council on Education.

INTERVENTIONS DEFINED, IMPLEMENTED, AND EVALUATED

Elizabeth Stage

Elizabeth Stage is director of critique and consensus at the National Research Council's National Committee on Science Education Standards and Assessment. In a distinguished career in the field of education, Dr. Stage previously was executive director of the California Science Project, which works out of the President's Office, University of California system, and deals with in-service programs for teachers, kindergarten through community college. Prior to that, she was associated with the Lawrence Hall of Science, University of California at Berkeley, for 10 years.

Dr. Stage received her undergraduate degree in chemistry from Smith College. She subsequently taught mathematics and science in middle school in Massachusetts and then earned a master's and doctorate in science education at Harvard. Her professional experience with K-12 is the basis of this presentation on the issues associated with interventions at the undergraduate level to enhance the participation of women in science and engineering.

A Brief History and Conceptual Framework

In 1978 at Berkeley, Lucy Sells coined the expression "critical filter" to describe the role that high school mathematics preparation plays in the lives of women and minorities who are seeking to become scientists and to work in mathematics-based fields. She approached the staff at the Lawrence Hall of Science and said, "This is a public problem and you are a public science center. What are you going to do about it?" Not only did the Lawrence Hall of Science respond to her findings, but the data and her interpretations provided a conceptual frame for a national response to a problem that had clear and far-reaching implications. Funding agencies responded to Sells' findings by focusing research on females and mathematics, engineering and science studies, and careers. Under Susan Chipman's leadership, the National Institute of Education funded a series of studies that investigated different

15

hypotheses and used different methodologies to begin to explain why young women were less likely to take elective mathematics courses, with a view to changing the situation once it was better understood. About a decade ago, we began to hear and act upon the findings of this research.

The result was a wealth of intervention programs in science, mathematics, and engineering targeted toward women and focused on improving attitudes and increasing interest and participation. Perhaps more importantly, the design of many of these intervention programs was based upon the recently developed research base. In fact, there was tremendous respect and collegiality and considerable interaction between and among the scholars and the practitioners. This close coupling of research and practice contributed to the way that intervention programs developed and were implemented and evaluated. An appropriate definition of an intervention program should reflect this research-practice connection: *Having identified a problem to solve, select and implement a strategy (either to change the situation or to compensate somehow for a situation that you cannot change) and then continually monitor to see if your strategy is successful.* The definition is, therefore, simple, straightforward, and empirical.

Defining a Problem

There is great diversity in the approach taken by intervention program designers, beginning with the way that the problem-to-be-solved is described. First, there is a tension between a recognition of the complexity of the situation and not being overwhelmed by it. A myriad of factors combine to influence a child's interest in science or mathematics studies and related careers. These include both cognitive and affective factors, which vary depending upon the age of the child. Other important influences originate in the support and educational system in which the child functions: school, home, extracurricular activities, peer, and the media, for example. Previous research has shown us that these factors tend to work in combination with each other; therefore, we know that a single intervention event is unlikely to change all of the factors involved. Rather, systemic change in a variety of areas is needed. It is unlikely, however, that one can attempt to simultaneously approach all of these problems. One must define a manageable problem, one on which we can reasonably hope to have impact. This is especially true for science-related intervention programs for females since, many times, the program staff are doing the program on a volunteer basis and have other primary job responsibilities.

Intervention Targets and Strategies

Individuals

The intervention program designer also must decide exactly where the "problem" lies: Do we need to change girls' attitudes and behaviors, or do we need to change the system, which is not serving their needs? Or is there a combination of these approaches that functions more effectively? Many programs target individuals as participants to approach the problem of "How can we keep talent in the pool?"

Programs for talented youth are an example of those designed to address that question; not all programs agree on where the "problem" lies. At one end of the spectrum is the Johns Hopkins program for recruiting mathematically talented youth. Individuals associated with the administration of that program periodically identify some genetic or other biological rationale for not having enough women in the program (for example, Benbow and Stanley, 1984).

At the other end of the spectrum is the work of Harvey Keynes at the University of Minnesota Talented Youth Mathematics Program. Dr. Keynes asked why there were not more girls in his program and what he could do about it. He examined the procedures used to recruit and select students for the program and then modified the procedures until he got the number of females that he felt represented an extensive tapping of the female talent pool. Next, he changed the course, teaching styles, and interaction patterns in the class until he reached an acceptable success rate of recruitment, achievement, and retention of young women in his program. He is using a very systematic approach to fixing the system and procedures in order to be successful—a very different approach toward cultivation of individual talent. A similar approach is being taken in the new federal initiative, National Science Scholars Program, which has designated that, from every Congressional District, one female and one male scholar will receive a scholarship for undergraduate study in a scientific discipline. This action demonstrates a commitment to the beliefs that talented males and females are in the population and it is our job (or in this case, the job of the politicians) to find them.

17

Teachers, Faculty, and Adult Leaders

Often those who begin programs targeted at individual females move their efforts to the faculty level, whether that is teachers, adult leaders, or supervisors. One of the most frequent forms of science-related intervention programs is in-service programs for K-12 teachers focusing on equity issues. The overall goal is to help teachers and schools to be more effective in increasing interest and motivation in science and mathematics among girls.

Research has shown, however, that women often enter science-related fields because of experiences outside school: being part of the science club, visiting the Exploratorium, and participating in organizations such as Girl Scouts of the USA or Girls Inc. (formerly Girls Clubs of America). It is very promising to see that the notion of adult leadership and influence has been expanded from school teachers to include adults in the community. The work of Girls Inc. (1990), the proliferation of programs working with parents such as Family Math (Stenmark et al., 1986), and the work of the American Association for the Advancement of Science (AAAS) with local Girl Scout leaders (Matyas, 1992) are examples of this trend. By working with women from the community who typically have not had opportunities to be successful in science, we create not only some new role models but also some agents of change in the community. That expansion of our vision from the conventional institutions to the informal community institutions is an important one.

Peers

Expanding our concept of important potential target groups for intervention should not stop with adults, but must also include peers. As we develop programs in mathematics, science, and engineering to attract young women, it is essential that we recognize that not all males are served well by the existing system either and that many young men leave the educational system with the same stereotypes about women that intervention programs have spent considerable effort to debunk among their female peers. The Women in Engineering Program at Purdue University, building on a long track record of successful work with women, has begun to work with the men in engineering at Purdue in order to create a climate in which *people* more comfortably interact. This is success at an institutional level, where each person takes responsibility for the success of all members of the group. However, it takes a fairly confident and mature program to initiate this type of effort; I would not recommend it as a first step!

18

Intervention Mechanisms:
Beyond Isolated Programs

In the AAAS report, *Investing in Human Potential: Science and Engineering at the Crossroads*, Marsha Matyas and Shirley Malcom (1991) provided a framework of analysis for the progression of intervention mechanisms that I've begun to describe above (see Figure 4-2, page 56). First, we find isolated projects, which are most effective for creating awareness, for getting people to collect data, and for sorting out problem definition. A good example of an isolated project is an Expanding Your Horizons conference at which a group of people volunteer a day of their time to act as science and engineering role models. During these conferences, young women can sample the vast variety of opportunities in math- and science-based fields of study and work. At such a conference, they can also learn that all scientists (or engineers, or mathematicians, etc.) do not look the same and that a person does not have to follow a set lifestyle in order to be successful. Such an activity can be a wonderful eye-opening or door-opening experience. It may sensitize a young woman to seeing things differently at school and to the benefits of attending summer enrichment activities. It helps to bring some women in the scientific community and their male supporters into contact with one another; this often leads to additional local projects and interventions for girls and women.

The next step in this progression is recognition that isolated and infrequent intervention activities will not accomplish larger- and longer-term goals. This often leads to more regular and frequent activities, often organized on a department level basis. These programs usually stem from the leadership of a department chair or dean. The new Women in Science Project at Dartmouth (Muller, 1991) is an example of this type of departmental commitment.

These activities often lead to the development of cross-departmental activities such as women's centers or women's studies departments. For example, strong Society of Women Engineers (SWE) and Association for Women in Science (AWIS) chapters may have the support of an administrator and from them there emerges a network of support and activities to increase the recruitment and retention of young women into science and engineering.

19

Often these networking activities succeed because they provide opportunities to both women professionals and students to get support and to give support to others. It is important in creating successful programs (especially those with volunteer role models) to provide both kinds of experience.

As we move up the coordination line, at some point, coordinated programs must give way to structural reform. Examples might be changes in policies related to how quickly a student must take his/her oral examinations after being admitted to candidacy or how much time a student is allowed to take to write a dissertation. As Matyas and Malcom (1991) point out, this maturing of intervention programs moves from individual commitment (that is, one inspired person who rallies people together and either obtains soft money or works on a volunteer basis) and *grows into* hard money, line item and institutional budgets, and a strong institutional commitment. This is essential to avoid the demise of a program solely associated with one committed person when that person is no longer available to administer it.

Monitoring Progress

Although the definition of an intervention program provided earlier clearly suggests that intervention programs must "continually monitor to see if [their] strategy is successful," in reality most intervention programs have not extensively evaluated their effectiveness. According to Malcom and Matyas' study of intervention programs housed at U.S. colleges and universities, only about half had done any kind of evaluation of their program activities. Rarely does one find comprehensive program evaluations including cost effectiveness analyses and assessment of longitudinal impact on participants, yet it is this kind of information that can continue to inform and expand the research base on which these projects were initially built. Current programs are doing a better job than did programs in the 1970s and 1980s at:

- building in more extensive evaluation plans that can inform the ongoing development and implementation of the program's activities (formative evaluation) and can determine whether the program's initial goals are being met (summative evaluation);
- developing more realistic time-lines for program implementation in order to allow the intervention program to be "up and running" before summative evaluation takes place; and
- securing funding to support these evaluation efforts.

20

Some intervention programs are developing evaluation plans that are more sophisticated—adapted to the specific intervention activities (for example, assessment of changes in teaching strategies) and to the particulars of the intervention situation (for example, informal, after-school settings versus in-class settings). In general, however, effective intervention program evaluation might be considered work-in-progress.

Challenges for the '90s

As the backdrop for future planning, we must consider the following: What is the problem that we want to solve? Do the kids or the system need "fixing"? If we just build young women's confidence and self-esteem a little, will they make it through the existing system? Or are there ways to create a more effective and supportive educational and professional environment that can better foster achievement and self-esteem among both women and men?

The American Association of University Women recently commissioned Wellesley College to conduct a study of precollege students. They looked at the drop in self-esteem during adolescence—a time when both boys and girls experience a drop in self-confidence. Among their findings were the following:

- For boys, 67 percent of those in elementary school expressed confidence in themselves. The percentage drops about 10 points, to 56 percent, at middle school and another 10 points, to 46 percent, at high school, for a total of 20 points from elementary to high school.
- Notable differences were found for girls: 65 percent of African American girls expressed self-confidence at the elementary level, 59 percent at middle school, and 58 percent at high school; in fact, they have a slight edge on males, on average. However, the confidence level for white girls goes from 55 percent expressing confidence in themselves at elementary school, down to 29 percent at middle school, and 22 percent at high school. Hispanic girls start out with a slight plus—68 percent of them are self-confident in elementary school, 54 percent in middle school, and 30 percent in high school (AAUW, 1991).

The Wellesley researchers did not break out this particular study by academic success level but, in general, high-achieving girls at adolescence face

21

considerable conflict between continuing to work for academic success (which is often perceived by peers as "nerdy") and giving in to pressures to suppress their academic talent in order to be more socially accepted, especially by their male peers. This phenomenon was described by Casserly in 1979 and is still regularly reported by school teachers and intervention program directors today. Certainly, at the undergraduate level, the self-confidence of high-achieving young women drops significantly compared to that of their male peers (Arnold, 1985).

This unsupportive adolescent climate suggests that every effort should be taken to support individuals and help them to retain their self-confidence and enthusiasm. The current climate is too treacherous to stop at the individual student level, however, so "fixing" females so they can survive the current system is a necessary but insufficient condition for success at any educational level.

Working to change curricula and teaching strategies is somewhat more systematic and has greater potential for systemic effects, since these factors (and the educators who implement them) are significant contributors to the development of individual student talent. It is essential that teachers be provided with curricula that acknowledge and support the contributions of scientists and engineers of both sexes and diverse racial/ethnic backgrounds and cultures. Curricular examples and analogies must be diverse to relate to this broad audience as well. And teaching strategies must be selected according to their effectiveness with students of differing learning styles.

A variety of successful model intervention programs working with teachers and schools are available. It is important to reiterate that *well-evaluated* programs that effect changes in teacher behaviors or in curriculum that benefit female and/or minority students generally benefit other key persons as well— white male students; teachers; the school, in general; and the community. This should not come as a surprise, especially for those in systems engineering: If one takes a careful look at a situation and tries to make it work better, it works better. It bears repeating, though, that analysis and evaluation are the keys to success.

We must expand our intervention efforts to include not only the school, but the community as well. As we work toward this goal, we must expand our definition of the word "community." Among the most disheartening reports from recently collected data is that black females are better served in programs that are for minorities than they are in programs targeted at women and that Hispanic women are virtually unserved by either the minority programs or the women's programs (Matyas and Malcom, 1991). We must rethink what we mean by an "outreach" program and must forge coalitions between those who coordinate outreach or intervention efforts and those who are leaders in the particular communities we hope to reach.

Beyond supporting individual students and teachers and creating a community of support, we also need to think about "fixing science" in the sense that Linda Wilson alluded to in her comments and that Evelyn Fox Keller (1985) writes about most eloquently. Stated most simply, Keller's position is that if you only change the students to fit the existing system, you have "Dress-For-Success" science, whereby students and professionals may look the part by wearing lab coats and conducting experiments but are not full members of the scientific community. In the short term this is not a bad strategy: at the University of California-Irvine, Eloy Rodriquez dresses migrant youngsters in lab coats and brings them into the laboratory. They put on the mantle of scientists, have their picture taken with the microscope with which they work, and develop a sense of tremendous pride. But dressing up for the occasion is not all that is required. The argument is that if enough women and/or minorities get into the scientific community, then we can fix the system. But if along the way we lose the talent and enthusiasm of so many young women and young men who could not survive the system, the price may be too high and the strategy an ineffective one.

Future Intervention:
Focus on Systemic Change

We must work at every level.
To date, we have made the least conscious effort to improve undergraduate programs, especially what the University of California system calls the "lower division" (the freshman and sophomore years). Data released by the Higher Education Research Institute (Green, 1989) show that the percentage of men intending to major in sciences at the undergraduate level fell from 14 percent in 1966 to 7 percent in 1988 (that is, by half). The percentage of women intending to major in sciences as undergraduates fell from 9 percent in 1966 to 5 percent in 1988. These drops in enrollment in undergraduate science courses have occurred despite committed efforts of

23

people both in California and across the nation. We can only imagine what the statistics would have been if no intervention programs had been instituted.

We must target more than just the transition points.

Many intervention strategies have targeted transition points to make sure that students get into the right college preparatory sequence in high school; they are admitted to the university; they seriously look at the majors that will lead to career opportunities; and they get into graduate programs. However, by focusing only on the transition points, we miss some very critical areas, including the lower division. A number of scientific societies have released reports stating that the lower division does not serve anyone well. It does not serve future scientists because it discourages some of our brightest people from staying. It does not encourage future science teachers because of the way it models teaching and learning science. It does not inspire the general public to think that science is something that they could possibly learn so our elementary teachers are discouraged from studying or teaching any science.

By looking at the whole system, it becomes apparent that there is plenty of room to effect change at every level. We need to think about where the problems lie. If we have the energy and determination to attack the problem at the structural level——the systemic level, the "We can really change science if we seek to" level——then we should try to do so, or at least have that as our ultimate goal. We must make this our aspiration because, if we keep on attempting to make everyone else as persistent as we are, progress will be on a very, very slow road.

Conclusion

In closing, I would like to comment about where I see success in science for women fitting into the overall context of what is going on in educational reform right now. Fortunately, current rhetoric has shifted from blaming the individual for his or her lack of success to looking to the system to take responsibility. The Mathematical Sciences Education Board (1989) slogan that "mathematics should be a pump rather than a filter" is an excellent one. The movement toward standards and assessment in both mathematics and science has the potential for great good or great harm. If equity issues are addressed as a key element of the standards and assessment movement, much good will be accomplished. To date, however, the area of assessment has received less attention in terms of equity issues. It needs our full attention now in terms of the national agenda of educational reform.

Finally, the social and political reform climate and its inattention to women are of concern. Most people who are not directly involved in equity education or science-related intervention programs believe that the problem has been solved. "Didn't we already take care of the women's issue?" is a frequent response to attempts to inform the larger community of the current status of the education and employment of females, particularly in the sciences and engineering. Instead, what has occurred is a masking of the issues, particularly at the K-12 level. After the report, *A Nation at Risk* (National Commission on Excellence in Education, 1983) was released, many states increased their high school graduation requirements so that more years of mathematics and science were required for high school graduation. Therefore, young women often were required to take the courses where gender differences in enrollment were previously seen. Gender differences in overall number of high school science and mathematics courses decreased but, upon closer examination, important differences between males and females remained. Females were still avoiding the highest-level options in science and mathematics: physics, calculus, and advanced chemistry. Therefore, the effect of the reforms was to raise the stakes for the most talented students, and females were still avoiding the courses that could be the real keys to success in undergraduate science, mathematics, and engineering programs. These differences are even more dramatic for whites versus minority group members.

Tackling the issues facing girls and women in mathematics, science, and engineering on a one-by-one basis and through isolated intervention programs is labor-intensive and provides for only slow and sporadic change. Attempting systemic change using these methods is virtually impossible. Collaborative strategies implemented by coalitions of administrators, faculty, and community leaders both within an institution and among institutions are needed to begin to build the ultimate intervention programs—the ones that can resolve the disparity in science, mathematics, and engineering for women and men, once and for all.

REFERENCES

Arnold, Karen D. 1985. *Retaining High-Achieving Women in Science and Engineering.* Invited presentation for the American Association for the Advancement of Science conference, "Women in Science and Engineering: Changing Vision to Reality." Ann Arbor, MI.

American Association of University Women (AAUW). 1991. *How Schools Shortchange Girls.* Washington, DC: AAUW.

Benbow, C. P. and J. C. Stanley. 1984. Reports. *Science* **226**(4679):1029.

Casserly, Patricia L. 1979. *Helping Able Young Women Take Math and Science Seriously in School.* Dubuque, IA: Kendall/Hunt.

Girls Inc. 1990. *The Power Project: Operation SMART.* New York: Girls Inc.

Green, Kenneth C. 1989. A profile of undergraduates in science. *American Scientist.* **77**(5):475-481.

Keller, Evelyn Fox. 1985. *Reflections on Gender and Science.* New Haven: Yale University Press.

Mathematical Sciences Education Board (MSEB) and Board on Mathematical Sciences (BMS). 1989. *Everybody Counts: A Report to the Nation on the Future of Mathematics Education.* Washington, DC: National Academy Press.

Matyas, Marsha Lakes. 1992. *Girl Scouts, Science, and Mathematics: Linkages for the Future—A Program for Adult Leader Training.* Report submitted to the Bush Foundation, St. Paul, MN. Washington, DC: American Association for the Advancement of Science.

_____, and Shirley M. Malcom. 1991. *Investing in Human Potential: Science and Engineering at the Crossroads.* Washington, DC: American Association for the Advancement of Science.

Muller, Carol B. 1991. Women in science: Changing attitudes and outcomes. *Directions* 6(1):2-5.

National Commission on Excellence in Education. 1983. *A Nation at Risk: The Imperative for Educational Reform.* Washington, DC: U.S. Government Printing Office.

Stenmark, Jean Kerr, Virginia Thompson, and Ruth Cossey. 1986. *Family Math.* Berkeley, CA: University of California Regents.

3

OVERVIEW: THE STATUS OF WOMEN IN SCIENCE AND ENGINEERING

Marsha Lakes Matyas

Dr. Matyas currently serves as the director of the Women in Science Program in the Directorate for Education and Human Resources Programs of the American Association for the Advancement of Science. Her research fields include factors affecting science and engineering interests and participation rates among women and minorities at both the precollege and undergraduate levels. Her current projects include work with local youth-serving organizations to increase girls' extracurricular science and mathematics activities and the development and implementation of teacher materials and training programs for use in bilingual (English-Spanish) K-8 science classrooms.

In order to set the stage for the five chapters of this report that focus on interventions in S&E education and employment, it is appropriate to look at the current statistics and research that define the problems that these interventions seek to resolve.

Undergraduate Level

In 1989, women earned 53 percent of the bachelor's degrees conferred in the United States. However, they earned only 39 percent of the bachelor's degrees conferred in science (excluding social sciences and psychology) and only 15 percent of the engineering bachelor's degrees awarded (see Figure 5-1, page 68). Within science, the percentage of degrees awarded to women varied by field. While women earned 46 percent of bachelor's degrees in mathematics and 45 percent of those in life sciences, they earned less than a third of the degrees awarded in physical science (31 percent, including chemistry), computer science (31 percent), and environmental science (25 percent) (National Science Board, 1991).

These numbers should not be viewed as milestones on an upward

27

TABLE 3-1: Intended Majors of High-Achieving Black and White High-School Seniors, 1990, by Sex (in percent)

Intended Major	White		Black	
	Male	Female	Male	Female
Total S&E	56	37	55	36
Total science	27	29	21	22
Math/statistics	3	3	2	2
Computer science	4	1	6	3
Physical science	4	2	2	1
Life science	4	8	3	4
Earth/environmental science	*	*	*	*
Psychology	1	5	*	5
Social science	4	7	3	5
Other	4	3	3	2
Total engineering	29	9	34	14

* < 1%.
NOTE: Percentages for "total science" may not equal the sum of individual fields because of rounding.
SOURCE: Adapted from National Science Board, *Science and Engineering Indicators* (10th Edition) (NSB 91-1), Washington, DC: U.S. Government Printing Office, 1991, pp. 207-210.

swing of science and engineering degrees awarded to women. Rather, the number of both U.S. citizen women and men earning degrees in science and engineering fields is on the decline. The number of degrees awarded to women in physical sciences peaked in 1987 at 4,837. Women's degrees peaked in environmental science in 1984, in life sciences in 1980, and in engineering in 1987.

A number of factors contribute to the lower number of undergraduate degrees in science and engineering awarded to women. The major factors involved are summarized below, but this should not be considered a complete treatment of a complex set of variables and studies:

● Recent K-12 science and mathematics education reform efforts have

TABLE 3-2: Student Perceptions of Problems in Undergraduate Teaching Methods, by Sex (in percent)

	Men	Women
Impersonality	12	20
Professors don't care about you	0	30
Can't develop relationship with professors	25	10
Professors have no time for students	12	20
Large classes have negative effect on grades	25	0
Too competitive, and too fast a pace	13	10
No time for questions in class	0	10
Faculty don't know how to teach	13	0

SOURCE: Nancy M. Hewitt and Elaine Seymour, *Factors Contributing to High Attrition Rates Among Science, Mathematics, and Engineering Undergraduate Majors,* Boulder, CO: University of Colorado, 1991.

increased the amount of science and mathematics that most students are required to take (Capper, 1988) and, consequently, female students are as likely to complete courses in Algebra I, Algebra II, Geometry, Trigonometry, Biology, Chemistry and Geology as are their male counterparts. However, young women are less likely to take the "final" courses that facilitate entry into science and engineering majors in college: physics and calculus (Nelson et al., 1992).

- Female students do not exhibit the same level of interest in science and engineering studies as do males (Table 3-1). Among 1990 high school seniors scoring above the 90th percentile on the mathematics portion of the SAT, women are only two-thirds as likely as men to go into science and engineering.

- Among those students who initially enroll in science and engineering, attrition has always been a problem, especially for women. According to a recent study of undergraduate students by Hewitt and Seymour (1991), women don't "switch" to other majors because they aren't prepared or don't make adequate grades. Rather, they often perceive the teaching methods used in undergraduate science, mathematics, and engineering courses as impersonal and uncaring (Table 3-2).

29

- Hewitt and Seymour's study also describes the alienation of students in general and how many aspiring female scientists and engineers feel alienated from the mainstream S&E community. Among female undergraduate students interviewed, "nearly all complained about the daily irritation of dealing with open (or thinly veiled) sexist remarks from their male peers, and with the inner stresses of feeling unwelcome and pressured" (p. 98).

- Finally, gender differences in financial aid for students are consistently found. Although the National Science Foundation reports that half of both male and female students depend upon "relatives" and "savings" for financial support and 27 percent of male and female students have grants or scholarships, more female (52 percent) than male (47 percent) students express "some" concern about financing their education and female students are more likely to see financial aid as a major concern (NSF, 1990).

Graduate and Postdoctoral Levels

Since 1980, women have represented about one-third of graduate enrollment in science and engineering disciplines, although this varies by field (NSF, 1990). Women's graduate enrollment in S&E tends to be concentrated in one of three fields—social sciences, psychology, and life sciences—while men tend to be concentrated in engineering programs (see Figure 5-1, page 68). In 1986, women earned 31 percent of all master's degrees conferred and 33 percent of all master's degrees conferred in science (excluding social science and psychology), but only 11 percent of master's degrees awarded in engineering (NSF, 1990).

The percentages of doctoral degrees awarded to women have increased significantly, particularly in certain S&E disciplines. For example, in 1950 only 4 percent of doctoral degrees in chemistry, 6 percent of those in mathematics, and 5 percent of those in physics were awarded to women. In 1990, those percentages were 24 percent, 18 percent, and 11 percent, respectively (Table 3-3). Women earning S&E doctoral degrees tend to be clustered in the life sciences.

Some of the factors leading to women's underrepresentation among graduate degree recipients are similar to those for the undergraduate level. First, the transition between undergraduate and graduate school is critical, yet

TABLE 3-3: Doctoral Degrees Awarded to Women, by Field, 1990

Field	Total Degrees	Degrees to Women Number	Percent
TOTAL, All Fields	36,027	13,061	36
Physical Science	5,859	1,068	18
Mathematics	892	158	18
Computer Science	704	110	16
Physics	1,392	149	11
Chemistry	2,102	502	24
Environmental Science	769	149	19
Engineering	4,892	414	8
Life Sciences	6,613	2,474	37
Biology	4,333	1,606	37
Health	960	595	62
Agriculture	1,320	273	28
Social Sciences	6,076	2,815	46
Psychology	3,267	1,906	58
Humanities	3,820	1,741	46
Language/Literature	1,308	746	57
Education	3,736	6,484	58
Professional/Other	813	2,283	36

SOURCE: Delores H. Thurgood and Joanne M. Weinmann, *Summary Report 1990: Doctorate Recipients from United States Universities*, Washington, DC: National Academy Press, 1991.

women do not make the transition as often as do men to earn master's degrees (NSF, 1990). For most S&E fields, the time required by women to earn a doctoral degree is no longer than the time required by men (NSF, 1990; see also Table 5-1, page 69). In physical science fields, women in doctoral programs are about as likely as men to receive financial support from the university and are only slightly more likely than their male peers to depend primarily on personal sources for support (Thurgood and Weinmann, 1991). However, in life sciences, 29 percent of women versus 20 percent of men depended primarily on personal sources of funds throughout their doctoral studies. Finally, the alienation that prevents full participation of

31

women at the undergraduate level is even stronger at the graduate level. Examples range from simply being "left out" of the intellectual process to disparaging remarks about women and blatant sexual harassment (Frazier-Kouassi et al., 1992). With the critical role played in the life and future success of graduate students by the departmental faculty (in particular the major adviser), the impact of even minimal alienation can be tremendous.

Employment

The National Science Foundation (1990) cites five major areas of difference between male and female scientists and engineers in the United States:

1   Numbers: Women are underrepresented in science and engineering compared to their participation in the U.S. work force (45 percent). In 1988 women comprised 16 percent of all scientists and engineers (30 percent of scientists; 4 percent of engineers).

2   Unemployment: The unemployment rate for women scientists and engineers in 1986 (2.7 percent) was more than double that of their male peers (1.3 percent). It was, however, considerably lower than the unemployment rate for all U.S. women (7.1 percent).

3   Underemployment: "Women scientists and engineers were three times as likely as men to report being underemployed in 1986: 6.3 percent versus 1.9 percent." In this case, NSF defines an underemployed person as one seeking an S&E position (who currently has a non-S&E job) or seeking a full-time rather than their current part-time S&E job.

4   Salaries: Women's yearly earnings are approximately three-fourths those of men's. "Their yearly earnings were also below those for men within individual S&E fields and—with few exceptions—at all levels of professional experience."

5   Years of Experience: Due to the recent increase of women entering S&E fields, women "on average, are younger and have fewer years of professional experience than their male colleagues." Nearly two-thirds of women in science and engineering versus only a quarter of men had less than 10 years of professional experience in 1986.

In addition to these general indicators of the status of women working in science and engineering, specific concerns can be detailed in each

32

of the major areas of their employment: academe, industry, and government. One concern common to all employment sectors is the existence of a "glass ceiling," defined by the U.S. Department of Labor (1991) as "those artificial barriers based on attitudinal or organizational bias that prevent qualified individuals from advancing upward in their organizations into management level positions." The Labor Department (1991) identified three such attitudinal and organizational barriers:

- Recruitment practices involving reliance on word-of-mouth and employee referral networking; the use of executive search and referral firms in which affirmative action/EEO requirements were not made known.
- Developmental practices and credential building experiences, including advanced education, as well as career enhancing assignments such as to corporate committees and task forces and special projects—which are traditional precursors to advancement—were often not as available to minorities and women.
- Accountability for Equal Employment Opportunity responsibilities did not reach to senior level executives and corporate decision makers.

Academe

Educational institutions are the leading employers of doctoral scientists and engineers in the United States (Vetter, 1989). In 1987 women comprised 17 percent of all doctoral scientists and engineers employed at educational institutions (Table 3-4). However, the percentage of women varies considerably by field from 2.4 percent in engineering to nearly 20 percent in the life sciences. Even higher percentages of women are found in psychology (31 percent) and the social sciences (30 percent).

As noted by Garrison Sposito in Chapter 6, academic women scientists and engineers face significant barriers in the tenure process. Two-thirds of women on S&E faculties do not have tenure versus 40 percent of male faculty members (see Figure 6-1, page 102). Furthermore, women progress up the academic ladder at a slower pace than do their male peers, even when matched for educational background, years of professional experience, and research productivity (CWSE, 1991; Brush, 1991).

Industry

Industrial employment and self-employment account for only 24

TABLE 3-4: Employed Women Doctoral Scientists and Engineers in Educational Institutions, by Field, 1989

Selected Fields	Total	Women	
		Number	Percent
All Fields	220,942	39,864	18.0
All Science*	195,981	39,185	20.0
Chemistry	15,074	1,861	12.3
Physics/Astronomy	13,825	640	4.6
Mathematics	11,614	1,116	9.6
Computer Science	6,349	689	10.9
Environmental Sciences	5,519	534	9.7
Biological Sciences	43,198	10,264	23.8
Engineering	24,961	679	2.7

*Includes social sciences and psychology.
SOURCE: Betty M. Vetter, *Professional Women and Minorities,* Washington, DC: Commission on Professionals in Science and Technology, 1992, p. 131.

percent of employed female doctoral scientists and engineers compared to 33 percent of men. As in academe, the percentage of women varies by field (Table 3-5), ranging from 2.5 percent in engineering to nearly 16 percent in life sciences. Data on industrial scientists and engineers at other degree levels are not generally available.

According to the National Science Foundation (1990), one estimate of the career development of scientists and engineers is the degree to which they have management responsibility. This is especially useful for those in industrial and government positions. In 1986 women scientists and engineers, in general, were less likely than their male counterparts to be primarily engaged in R&D management (see Figure 7-1, page 120). This difference was

TABLE 3-5: Employed Women Doctoral Scientists and Engineers in Industrial/Self-Employed Positions, 1989

		Women	
Selected Fields	Total	Number	Percent
All Fields	145,148	19,485	12.1
All Science*	103,189	18,148	15.8
Chemistry	25,799	2,200	7.5
Physics	6,243	257	3.9
Mathematics	2,105	285	11.3
Computer Science	11,483	1,318	9.7
Environmental Sciences	6,266	437	5.3
Life Sciences	23,572	4,303	15.9
Engineering	41,959	1,337	2.5

*Includes social sciences and psychology.
SOURCE: Unpublished data, 1989 Survey of Doctorate Recipients, National Science Foundation and National Research Council.

greatest in physical science (60 percent of men versus 40 percent of women) and in aeronautical/astronautical engineering (68 percent of men versus 25 percent of women)(NSF, 1990). While some might attribute these differences to the aggregation of all individuals in a discipline, no matter their length of work experience, it is worth noting that in the other fields of science and engineering, in which aggregate numbers are also reported, differences in the proportion of men and women in R&D management are more slight: they range from a difference of 1 percent (psychology: 15 percent for women and 14 percent for men; electrical/electronics engineering: 48 percent for women and 47 percent for men) to 9 percent (environmental science: 35 percent for men and 26 percent for women).

In terms of salary, women in industry earn similar or better starting salaries than men at the bachelor's level in chemistry and physics and at the bachelor's and master's degree levels in chemical engineering. At the Ph.D. level, however, men make higher starting salaries in chemical engineering and at most levels of experience in chemistry and physics (Babco, 1990).

Federal Government

The federal government employs over 200,000 scientists and engineers, primarily in eight major agencies and departments. Among doctoral scientists and engineers, the federal government is the third largest employer (29,710 employed in 1987) but the fourth largest employer of women (3,588), following educational institutions, industry, and hospitals/clinics (3,719). As Dix summarizes in Chapter 8,

> Across all degree levels, the employment of women scientists and engineers by the federal government varies by discipline, from a low of 3.0 percent in agronomy to 50.5 percent in sociology. But, in general, the rate of employment is much lower than that of men.

Male scientists and engineers employed by federal agencies are more than twice as likely as females to be supervisors or managers (Table 3-6). Salaries of male and female scientists employed by government agencies differ by sex in certain fields and occupational categories. For instance, male scientists working in research and development for the government in 1987 earned $45,802, on average, compared to women's $41,249 (Vetter, 1989). Among government chemists, men earned higher salaries at every degree level, including the Ph.D. Some of the salary differences are attributed to the greater number of years' experience that men, in general, have in these fields. However, recent studies indicate that part of the difference is due to the "glass ceiling" that can stymie the promotion of women beyond a certain GS level.

Summary

According to Alan Fechter, executive director of the National Research Council's Office of Scientific and Engineering Personnel, "It is not just a question of supply and demand but it is a matter of morals and ethics: it is not right in a society such as ours that women and underrepresented

TABLE 3-6: Management/Supervisory Status of Federal Scientists and Engineers, by Sex, 1987

Status	Men		Women	
	Number	Percentage	Number	Percentage
Supervisor/manager	55,378	29.5	3,801	12.6
Nonmanagement/ nonsupervisor	127,587	68.1	25,750	85.6
Status unknown	4,554	2.4	547	1.8
Total	187,519	100.0	30,098	100.0

SOURCE: Betty M. Vetter, *Professional Women and Minorities,* Washington, DC: Commission on Professionals in Science and Technology, 1989, p. 113.

minorities do not play as strong a role as white men in the very important enterprise of science and technology."

Understanding the problems that lead to the underrepresentation of women in science and engineering is a necessary first step in moving to alleviate that problem, but it is not sufficient. While we need to understand better the particular obstacles that prevent women from entering careers in science and engineering, we also need to continue, at the same time, to develop and implement programs that do something about removing those obstacles and increasing women's participation in science and engineering. There is no one unique formula for developing such programs. Furthermore, the development of new programs is made very difficult by current funding constraints at all levels of government and in the private sector. A clearinghouse that would collect and share information about programs that work is needed to facilitate the task of improving the participation of women. The development of the information base for such a clearinghouse was an underlying incentive for holding the National Research Council's Conference on Science and Engineering Programs. The idea is to share information about the effectiveness of programs so that we can make the best use of the limited resources that are currently available to achieve the objective of increasing the participation of women in the S&E work force. The paucity of information that would enable us to distinguish programs that work from those that do not work provides the basis for seeking more and better evaluation efforts.

REFERENCES

Babco, Eleanor L. 1990. *Salaries of Scientists, Engineers, and Technicians.* Washington, DC: Commission on Professionals in Science and Technology.

Brush, Stephen G. 1991. Women in science and engineering. *American Scientist* 79:404-19.

Capper, J. 1988. *State Educational Reforms in Mathematics, Science and Computers: A Review of the Literature.* Washington, DC: Center for Research Into Practice.

Committee on Women in Science and Engineering (CWSE). 1991. *Women in Science and Engineering: Increasing Their Numbers in the 1990s.* Washington, DC: National Academy Press.

Frazier-Kouassi, Susan, Oksana Malanchuk, Patricia Shure, David Burkham, Patricia Gurin, Carol Hollinshead, Donald J. Lewis, Patricia Soellner-Younce, Homer Neal, and Cinda-Sue Davis. 1992. *Women in Mathematics and Physics: Inhibitors and Enhancers.* Ann Arbor: The University of Michigan.

Hewitt, Nancy M., and Elaine Seymour. 1991. *Factors Contributing to High Attrition Rates Among Science, Mathematics, and Engineering Undergraduate Majors.* Boulder, CO: University of Colorado.

National Science Board. 1991. *Science and Engineering Indicators* (10th Edition) (NSB 91-1). Washington, DC: U.S. Government Printing Office.

National Science Foundation (NSF). 1990. *Women and Minorities in Science and Engineering* (NSF 90-301). Washington, DC: NSF.

Nelson, Barbara H., Iris R. Weiss, and Larry E. Conaway. 1990. *Science and Mathematics Education Briefing Book* (Volume II). Chapel Hill, NC: Horizons Research, Inc.

Thurgood, Delores H., and Joanne M. Weinmann. 1991. *Summary Report 1990: Doctorate Recipients from United States Universities.* Washington, DC: National Academy Press.

U.S. Department of Labor. 1991. *A Report on the Glass Ceiling Initiative.* Washington, DC: U.S. Government Printing Office.

Vetter, Betty M. 1992. *Professional Women and Minorities.* Washington, DC: Commission on Professionals in Science and Technology.

_____. 1989. *Professional Women and Minorities.* Washington, DC: Commission on Professionals in Science and Technology.

EDUCATION

Jennifer Lowry and Max Hanson make a project presentation in a Dartmouth College engineering sciences class on control theory. (Photo: John Douglas, Flying Squirrel Graphics)

Scholarship students supported by the National Action Council for Minorities in Engineering, Inc. (NACME) participate in an under-graduate laboratory experience.
(Photo: Steve Satori, Syracuse University)

4

PROMOTING UNDERGRADUATE STUDIES
IN SCIENCE AND ENGINEERING

Marsha Lakes Matyas

Dr. Matyas, director of the Women in Science Program in the Directorate for Education and Human Resources programs of the American Association for the Advancement of Science (AAAS), has examined student interest and enrollment in and attrition from science and engineering studies through a series of studies and papers over the last 10 years at AAAS and Purdue University. Information in this chapter that supplements the conference deliberations is drawn primarily from that research. In particular, she presents findings from the 1991 AAAS study and report, Investing in Human Potential: Science and Engineering at the Crossroads.

Identifying and Defining the Problem

As shown in Figure 4-1, in general, women tend to earn baccalaureates in psychology, the social sciences, and the life sciences while men most often pursue bachelor's degrees in engineering, the social sciences, and the life sciences. For more than 20 years, U.S. higher education institutions have recognized that special efforts are necessary to increase the gender and racial/ethnic diversity of undergraduate science and engineering (S&E) majors, especially in those subfields where they are present only in very small percentages. In general, progress has been made from 1980 to 1989, with the overall percentage of baccalaureates awarded to women increasing in both science and engineering. Efforts to enhance women's participation have been targeted at a variety of potential problem areas:

- generating interest in and prerequisite skills for S&E studies among female and/or minority students (Malcom, 1983; Matyas, 1987, 1988);
- converting precollege interests into matriculation with intent to major in an S&E field; and
- preventing attrition among S&E majors, especially attrition due to

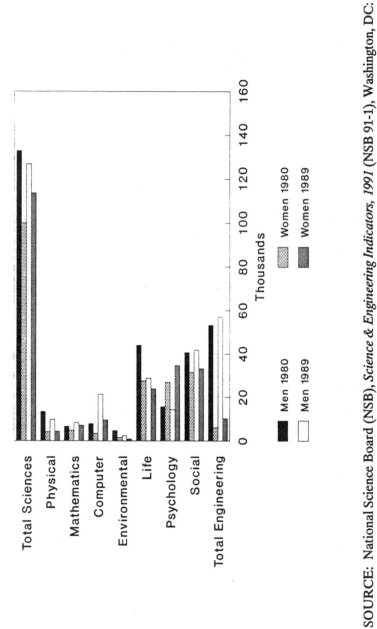

SOURCE: National Science Board (NSB), *Science & Engineering Indicators, 1991* (NSB 91-1), Washington, DC: NSB, 1992, p. 235.

Figure 4-1. Percentage of bachelor's degrees awarded in science and engineering, 1980 and 1989, by sex.

lack of adequate financial aid (Matyas, 1987, 1988; Malcom, 1983).

Unfortunately, many institutions' selection of problem areas to target are not based upon actual data pinpointing specific problems at their institutions. According to a recent study by the American Association for the Advancement of Science (AAAS), only 55 percent of the 276 U.S. colleges and universities participating in the study routinely calculated graduation or attrition rates for undergraduate students in all majors (Matyas and Malcom, 1991). Even fewer institutions calculated these rates separately for women (42 percent) or racial/ethnic minorities (44 percent). Therefore, institutional efforts may or may not be specifically focused on the problem faced by the particular institution.

By closely monitoring student progress through the undergraduate educational system, institutions can pinpoint whether underrepresented groups are or are not being recruited into S&E studies from secondary schools, having academic and/or social success in the first year of studies, and/or persisting in S&E studies after the initial semesters. Reasons for attrition from science and engineering (and subsequent solutions) differ at each of these levels, and these issues must be examined by specific S&E fields.

Selecting Solutions

Having pinpointed the likely target areas for intervention, institutional personnel must then decide what types of strategies to use to increase recruitment and/or retention in these three areas. Although the focus of the National Research Council's Committee on Women in Science and Engineering (CWSE) is on programs beginning at the undergraduate level, it is appropriate to insert here a brief review of the types of precollege efforts in operation for two reasons. First, many of the effective undergraduate recruitment and retention efforts by colleges and universities are grounded in outreach efforts at the precollege level. Second, research on precollege efforts provides useful information about the development and improvement of efforts at the undergraduate and graduate levels. Table 4-1 includes listings of target groups and program models for intervention at the precollege level. Briefly, recruitment efforts at the precollege level tend to introduce students to science and engineering careers, to the specific sponsoring institution, and to the academic courses, skills, and extracurricular activities needed to succeed

TABLE 4-1: Precollege Intervention Target Groups and Program Models

---

<u>Programs for Students</u>
Career Days/Fairs
Field Trips
Test-taking Skills Training
Academic Enrichment Programs
- After-school Workshops/Tutoring Programs
- Saturday Academies
- Summer Workshops
- Computer Camps
- University/College Accelerated Programs
- Academic Contests
Internships and Summer Jobs

<u>Programs for Teachers</u>
Academic Enrichment Programs (content and/or skills)
Science Resource Programs for Schools

<u>Programs for Parents</u>
Workshops and Courses
Career Days/Fairs

SOURCE: Marsha Lakes Matyas, *Intervention Programs in Mathematics and Science for Precollege Females: Program Types and Characteristics,* invited research report and presentation for the Bush Foundation Board of Directors, St. Paul, MN, 1988.

in science and engineering studies. They may also provide students with summer residential experiences in academic studies and research. Retention efforts range broadly from scholarships and internships to multi-year programs that involve students on a daily or weekly basis. Each of these program types has different goals and different levels of activity. As shown in Table 4-2, precollege efforts target both behaviors and attitudes of participants; the same is usually true of undergraduate intervention programs. Previous studies have identified some characteristics common to many effective precollege and undergraduate S&E intervention programs—that is, those that have under-

TABLE 4-2: Attitudes and Behaviors Affected by Precollege Program Activities

Attitudes/perceptions of*	Career Days	Field Trips	Testing Skills	Student Academic Enrichment	Internship	Teacher Academic Enrichment	Resources for School	Parent Workshop
students	✓	✓	✓	✓	✓	✓	✓	✓
parents	✓			✓				✓
school personnel	✓	✓				✓	✓	
Behaviors of								
● students								
academic performance			✓	✓		✓	✓	
test scores			✓	✓				
course selection	✓			✓	✓	✓	✓	✓
career selection	✓	✓		✓	✓	✓	✓	✓
extracurricular activities	✓	✓		✓	✓	✓		✓
● teachers/school personnel								
teaching strategies						✓	✓	
curricula						✓	✓	
encouraging students	✓					✓	✓	
● parents	✓			✓				✓

* Attitudes and perceptions include interest in science/math/engineering courses and careers, motivation, self-confidence, and expectations of success.
NOTE: The effects of teacher enrichment programs and parent workshops on student attitudes and behaviors are due to changes in teacher or parent attitudes and behaviors.
SOURCE: M. L. Matyas, *Intervention Programs in Mathematics and Science for Precollege Females: Program Types and Characteristics,* invited research report and presentation for the Bush Foundation Board of Directors, St. Paul, MN, 1988.

47

gone evaluation which proved that programmatic goals had been achieved (Malcom, 1983; Clewell and Ficklen, 1986; George et al., 1987; Matyas and Malcom, 1991):

- Goals are well-defined.
- A plan has been developed for evaluating the program's effectiveness.
- Strategies are based on current educational research findings and the program does not depend upon a single strategy for success.
- Participants are recruited from diverse racial/ethnic groups and have input into the design and implementation of the program activities.
- The program has strong support from and involvement of the sponsoring university's faculty and administration through group mentoring programs, advisory boards, laboratory visits, and/or research experiences for students.
- The program includes multi-year involvement with participants, strong academic components, daily or weekly contact with students, strong peer support networks, low or no fees for participation (or readily available financial aid), hands-on (laboratory) activities, inquiry approaches, cooperative learning situations, residential experiences for participants such as overnights, bridge programs, and summer programs where appropriate, and involvement of role models from both academe and industry.
- Outreach activities include activities with parents and teachers as well as students and have follow-up components for all three groups.

Although no program has all of these characteristics, effective programs tend to have many of them.

Program Highlights

A number of S&E programs at the undergraduate level were highlighted during the CWSE conference, representing many of the S&E program types listed in Table 4-3. Those described below are examples of the many efforts occurring around the country. The examples are far from a comprehensive listing of current intervention efforts at the undergraduate level. Rather, they provide a sample of the diverse approaches taken by higher education institutions, professional associations, federal agencies, private industry, and others to address the underrepresentation of women and minorities in science and engineering (see also Appendix Table A-1).

48

TABLE 4-3: Types of Undergraduate Intervention Programs

General Programs
- Retention program (usually for "at-risk" students—that is, those who are most likely to withdraw from either a particular academic major or the institution for either academic or non-academic reasons)
- Recruitment/admissions programs (all fields)
- Tutoring and study skills centers (courses)
- Activities through the office of women's and/or minority affairs

Science and Engineering Programs
- Recruitment programs
- Comprehensive retention programs
- Support for student research involvement [for example, Minority Access to Research Careers (MARC) and Minority Biomedical Research Support (MBRS)]
- Scholarships and forgivable loans
- Bridge programs (summer transition from high school to college)
- Mentoring activities and student chapters of professional associations
- Science/mathematics learning centers and skills improvement programs
- Internships/summer work experience

SOURCE: Marsha Lakes Matyas and Shirley M. Malcom, *Investing in Human Potential: Science and Engineering at the Crossroads,* Washington, DC: American Association for the Advancement of Science, 1991.

Recruitment Programs/
Comprehensive Retention Programs
    Effective recruitment efforts are often combined with retention efforts in the form of larger, more comprehensive programs that interact with students over a number of years. One well-established example of this type of effort is the Women In Engineering Program (WIEP) at Purdue University. Established in 1974, the program targets women in engineering. Recruitment activities for elementary, middle, and high school students include work with local Girl Scouts, essay contests, outreach speakers for schools, summer

49

camps, videos, on-campus career days, and scholarships for incoming freshmen. Retention efforts include an introductory "Women in Engineering" course for freshmen; a buddy system, which pairs female upperclassmen with incoming freshmen; special plant trips and shadow programs, in which students follow practicing engineers during a typical work day; and seminars for female seniors preparing to enter the work place. As a result, the recruitment and retention statistics on women enrolled in engineering at Purdue are higher than national averages. For example, the retention rate for women has risen from 25 percent in 1974 to 55 percent in 1991, equal to that of men majoring in engineering at Purdue (Daniels, 1990).

Although programs of this type are less often found in schools of science, a notable example is the Douglass Project for Rutgers Women in Math, Science and Engineering at Douglass College. In addition to utilizing some of the recruitment and retention strategies noted above, the Douglass College program makes science and engineering a "live-in" experience by coordinating the admission to and activities of a residence hall for 100 undergraduate and graduate women majoring in science, mathematics, or engineering. Special programs at the residence hall are open to non-residents as well.

Student Research Involvement

The National Institutes of Health (NIH) Minority Access to Research Careers (MARC) program was established in 1972; its Honors Undergraduate Research Training Program provides grants to junior and senior honors students at minority institutions. The overall goal is to increase the number of minority students who enter doctoral studies in biomedicine. In addition to receiving stipends, tuition, fees and travel funds, students receive research training, participate in honors courses and seminars, and spend summers conducting research at prominent research institutions. Currently, the program is being expanded to include freshman and sophomore students. The NIH also supports the involvement of minority students in research through its Minority Biomedical Research Support (MBRS) program. Evaluations of both the MARC and MBRS programs highlight their effectiveness in recruiting members of racial/ethnic minority groups into biomedical careers (Garrison and Brown, 1985). However, many studies of the effectiveness of programs open to both women and men do not evaluate the extent of the programs' effectiveness separately for women and men. For instance, although women comprised 55 percent of the respondents to the MARC survey (Garrison and Brown, 1985), analyses of the extent to which women

50

participate in the program and earn advanced degrees in biomedical sciences were not undertaken.

The Howard Hughes Medical Institute Undergraduate Scholars Program involves undergraduate students in summer and academic year research experiences in biology. Minority students are especially recruited for this program.

Scholarships and Forgivable Loans

AT&T funds undergraduate scholarships in the fields of engineering, computer science, mathematics, and physical science for both minorities and women through two programs: the Engineering Scholarship Program (ESP) and the Dual Degree Scholarship Program (DDSP). The ESP makes about 15 new awards each year, providing 60 students annually with full tuition, fees, books, and room and board for four years to maintain a steady state of 60. It also provides each student with a summer job and a mentor. The DDSP offers similar benefits for minority students attending one of the Historically Black Colleges and Universities (HBCUs) that comprise the Atlanta University Center for three years. These students later transfer to schools of engineering at partner institutions for the final two years of study.

The California State University (CSU) at Los Angeles has a variety of programs for undergraduate students, including a Forgivable Loan Doctoral Incentive Program to encourage undergraduate women and minorities to pursue doctoral degrees in targeted disciplines. Students receive up to $10,000 per year for three years to attend the graduate institution of their choice. After graduation, the loan recipient can reduce the loan amount by 20 percent for each year of service as a faculty member at one of the 20 CSU campuses. In existence since 1987 and funded by the California State Lottery, the Forgivable Loan Doctoral Incentive Program has been evaluated by an external group, which concluded that the program is effective. In fact, in the four years, 1987-1990, 44 students participating in this program have received their doctorates, and 26 of them are employed as CSU faculty. Furthermore, of the 469 students enrolled in the program since 1987, only 18 have dropped out of their Ph.D. program.

Bridge Programs

The CSU system also conducts a summer bridge program to assist students in transition from high school or community college to the university. The program targets minority students and involves over 2,500 students each year on 19 campuses. Program activities include diagnostic testing, English and mathematics instruction, academic advising, and orientation to university life. The program has raised the one-year retention rate for participating students higher than the systemwide average and has improved two-year retention rates for those students most at risk of dropping out.

Mentoring Activities

The Association for Women in Science is currently coordinating a mentoring program through its 47 local chapters (Bird, 1991). The program is designed to increase student interest in and enthusiasm for science careers and to encourage talented students to remain in the educational pipeline by providing them with a clearer understanding of careers in science. Chapter mentoring activities provide a support structure for women already committed to a science major; introduce options in the sciences to students who may not have previously considered a science major; and provide encouragement, support, and assistance to undergraduate and graduate women science students. Mentors and chapter activities address a wide range of issues and topics that are critical to successful professional development in general, as well as specific issues that are of particular relevance to women. Activities include receptions for undergraduate and graduate students, role model panels, research seminars, career development seminars, travel awards for students to attend professional meetings, pairing of mentors with students to promote a variety of one-on-one interactions, and paid and unpaid laboratory internships. One example of an AWIS mentoring program is that of the Dartmouth Chapter, which, in conjunction with the Women in Science Program, reaches 25 percent of freshmen women.

Undergraduate mentoring activities are frequently found in the form of "Big Sister" programs in which junior and senior undergraduate women mentor freshmen women in science or engineering. These programs are being successfully implemented at Purdue University (as described above) and as part of the comprehensive effort by the Women in Engineering (WIE) Initiative at the University of Washington. Such programs are no doubt also operating successfully at other universities, both in schools of engineering and schools of science. Student chapters of organizations such as the Society of Women Engineers often coordinate these activities, as they do at Purdue University.

Augmenting Course Activities

The Emerging Scholars Program (ESP) at the University of Texas-Austin is an excellent example of how high expectations can facilitate achievement and persistence. Based on the work of Uri Treisman, director of the Dana Center for Mathematics and Science Education at the University of Texas at Austin, the ESP is one of 125 nationwide that involve students from diverse racial/ethnic groups and mathematics backgrounds in an intensive discussion section and coordinated group work attached to a standard calculus lecture (Wheeler, 1992). ESP is an honors program that serves a unique group of students: those who have "shown promise for achievement in mathematics and science based on their high school work" (McCaffrey, 1991, p. 3) but who earned SAT scores 100 points lower, on average, than is typical of honor students. Three-quarters of the students in the program are black or Hispanic, and most come from small town/rural or inner city schools and are not accustomed to intense academic competition. The program stresses high academics and, according to evaluation results, accomplishes its goals. While fewer than one third of black and Hispanic students at the university typically receive As or Bs in calculus, 90 percent of the minority students enrolled in ESP do so (McCaffrey, 1991). Furthermore, by the end of their third year, 86 percent of ESP students are still enrolled as science or engineering majors, compared to only 40-50 percent of all students at the university who originally enrolled as science or engineering majors. Although these comparison samples are not identical, the dramatic differences in performance and persistence between minority students in the ESP and those who are taking calculus are strong indicators of the effectiveness of this program. As the program (now only in its fourth year) continues, more comprehensive evaluations will be conducted.

Internships and Summer Work

Internships and summer work experiences are often found as components of comprehensive programs (such as Purdue's WIEP), as a part of a scholarship or fellowship (for example, the AT&T scholarships), or as a portion of student research involvement efforts (such as MARC or the Howard Hughes Program). Additional examples include the AT&T Summer Research Program for Women and Minorities for undergraduate juniors and seniors; the Argonne National Laboratory Science and Engineering Research Semester, which is designed to encourage undergraduates to pursue advanced degrees; and the Hewlett-Packard Student Employment and Educational Development (SEED) program, which emphasizes the participation of women and minorities in engineering and computer science. The Argonne and Hewlett-Packard programs are open to all undergraduates in science and engineering.

53

Implementing Programs

At the conference held by CWSE in 1991, participants discussed the process of developing and implementing program models at various institutions. Five steps in this process relate specifically to undergraduate programs:

1   After clearly defining the goals and the planned strategies, support should be developed among top administration, faculty, and students. These supporters should have input into the design of the intervention programs.
2   Specific and measurable goals should be set, and both formative (ongoing) and summative (end goal) evaluation plans should be developed.
3   Appropriate funds should be secured for the program. These funds may be external, internal, or (more commonly) a combination of both. The funding mix will often be different at initiation and in the steady state.
4   Participants should represent diverse racial/ethnic groups and geographic areas.
5   Program activities should be revised, based upon evaluation results.

The steps for implementing model programs at other levels of the education/employment pipeline are discussed in subsequent chapters of this report.

Beyond Intervention:
Rethinking the Undergraduate Experience

Science and engineering intervention programs for undergraduate students were developed originally as "stop gap" measures to provide additional information, encouragement, and financial and social support for female and minority undergraduate students to pursue degrees in nontraditional areas. The ultimate goal has been to increase the flow of these underrepresented students through the S&E undergraduate educational process until they are no longer perceived (and perceive themselves) as nontraditional students. This strategy has been effective to a certain extent (see, for instance, Hewitt and Seymour, 1991; Muller, 1991; and Wheeler, 1992). However, nearly all intervention strategies to date have been focused on increasing the nontraditional student's skills at surviving the existing undergraduate educational system. They have rarely focused on changing the system itself.

Successful intervention programs provide considerable insight into the direction in which the overall system should move to provide a better educational experience for all students. First of all, as shown by recent studies and discussed during the 1991 conference, institutions must move forward in this process. For example, Matyas and Malcom (1991) note that intervention efforts must evolve from isolated intervention efforts to structural reform; from the commitment of individual program directors and involved faculty and administrators to an institution-wide commitment; and from isolated projects supported primarily by external funds or volunteer services to line-item budgets that support a variety of on-going activities (Figure 4-2).

During the conference, Paula Rayman of Wellesley College, a women's college, described the three institutional factors at Wellesley that create a "culture of success for women in the sciences" (Rayman, 1991). First, student-faculty partnerships are facilitated through small class size and opportunities for research experience. Second, students "see women being successful every day in all the sciences" since over 50 percent of the science faculty are women. Third, science is integrated into the liberal arts agenda: all students are required to take three science courses, one of which must be a laboratory course, in order to graduate.

Furthermore, in order to develop this positive attitude toward diversity, a number of institutional personnel must be involved. According to Theodore J. Crovello of California State University, Los Angeles, moving from isolated projects to a coordinated campus intervention effort involves a variety of campus personnel and activities as well as external contacts (Table 4-4). He attributes the success of their programs to the positive involvement of faculty:

> Cal State—L.A. programs succeed in general because of a widespread conviction that is translated into action: that a capable faculty committed to providing underrepresented students with deep learning experiences in modern science and engineering as well as with caring academic counseling CAN [sic] help such students achieve confidence, academic excellence and success (Crovello, 1991).

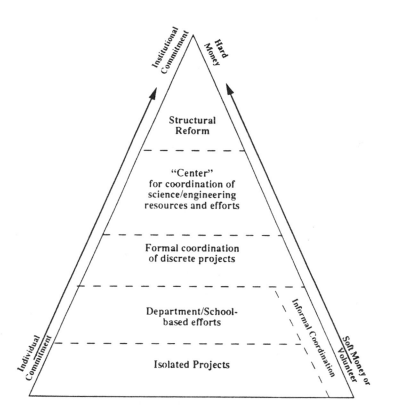

Structural
Reform

- - - - -

"Center"
for coordination of
science/engineering
resources and efforts

- - - - - - - - -

Formal coordination
of discrete projects

- - - - - - - - - - - -

Department/School-
based efforts

- - - - - - - - - - - - - - -

Isolated Projects

Institutional Commitment

Hard Money

Individual Commitment

Informal Coordination

Soft Money or Volunteer

SOURCE: Matyas, Marsha Lakes, and Shirley M. Malcom, *Investing in Human Potential: Science and Engineering at the Crossroads,* Washington, DC: American Association for the Advancement of Science, 1991.

Figure 4-2. Model for the evolution of intervention programs.

It should be emphasized that this type of climate change involves the participation of both male and female faculty members acting in their roles as educators, researchers, advisers, mentors, administrators, and role models. If the burden of change lies only with women faculty, then the chances for systemwide change are limited.

TABLE 4-4: Components of a Campus-Wide Coordination of Intervention Efforts

Campus People & Components	Essential Functions
Students	Quality teaching and research
Faculty	Successful grant proposals
Staff	Effective mentoring
Campus administrators	Effective program administration
Intervention program coordinator	Effective communication within and among programs
Intervention program advisory council	Positive program visibility
	Effective outreach on and off campus
	Constructive evaluation
External Components	Essential record keeping within
Funding agencies	and among programs
Corporations	Special events
School systems	
Community colleges	
Professional organizations	

SOURCE: Theodore J. Crovello, *Programs That Work: The Cal-State Los Angeles Experience and a General Campus Model*, paper presented at the National Research Council conference, "Science and Engineering Programs: On Target for Women?," Irvine, CA, November 4-5, 1991.

The second key point participants at the 1991 conference identified in the evolutionary process was a change in how institutions view student persistence and attrition. Currently, many science and engineering departments in the United States utilize a "weeding" strategy—allowing and even encouraging students to withdraw from science and engineering studies by setting high "failure" levels. Institutions and departments must direct educational programs toward "cultivation" of students rather than "weeding." This change in approach would prevent talented students from leaving science or engineering majors due to initial deficiencies in skills.

Thirdly, participants noted that many institutions that have traditionally hosted a number of isolated intervention programs are ready to take the next step toward coordination of those programs. Two examples are especially noteworthy. First, California State University, Los Angeles, has 15 successful science and engineering programs designed to create a total pipeline perspective that follows students from precollege through doctoral studies. Activities are coordinated through a Science, Engineering, and Mathematics (SEM) Council and SEM Coordinator. Similarly, the University of Puerto Rico established a Resource Center for Science and Engineering in 1980. This center focuses on a holistic approach to science education, working with disadvantaged students throughout the K-16 S&E pipeline. In 1989, the Center, along with the Commonwealth Department of Education and a number of two-year and four-year colleges and universities, established the Comprehensive Regional Center for Minorities (CRCM), whose objective is:

> to expand science education and science and engineering research efforts throughout the entire island. Components of the CRCM programs include precollege and undergraduate initiatives. Subcomponents of the precollege components are intervention programs for tracking talented students in grades 7-12 to enriched academic programs; continuing education for precollege teachers; an institute for the development of master teachers; and school-based programs. The undergraduate component of CRCM includes student enrichment programs; undergraduate student education development; and faculty development (George, 1991).

The final step in this evolutionary process—structural reform—has not been attained by any of the institutions represented at the 1991 conference, nor in any of the 276 institutions participating in the AAAS study:

> Not found among any of the institutions was a model of *structural reform* where the structure of courses, pedagogical techniques, institutional climate, and system for recruitment and retention co-existed with a supportive administrative structure, that is, where the regular support of departments and programs provided mechanisms to support the achievement of all students committed to education in

science and engineering. Only by moving from ancillary activities aimed at helping students survive the current educational climate to changing the climate in which the students are educated can we . . . significantly [affect] the participation of women, minorities, people with disabilities and, indeed, all students in science, mathematics, and engineering (Matyas and Malcom, 1991).

As discussed by conference participants, one catalyst for this reform may be the changing composition of the student body and faculty. As women and minorities begin to reach a "critical mass" within departments, they will begin to have input into and influence on the reform process. As described later in this report by Linda Wilson (see page 169), this reform can occur incrementally and will benefit both women and men at the faculty and student levels.

Undergraduate Programs: On Target for Women?

As noted earlier, there are a number of models for different types of S&E programs. But one must examine them with two questions in mind. First, how frequently are these types of efforts found at U.S. colleges and universities, and how often are they targeted toward women? The AAAS study mentioned earlier found few programs directly targeting female undergraduate students. In fact, less than 10 percent of the over 300 programs identified were targeted at women while 51 percent of the programs were targeted at minority students.

Second, are the types of programs suited to the barriers women encounter in science and engineering studies and careers? In the AAAS study, the types of programs targeted at women were different in focus from those targeted at minority students (it is recognized that the recruitment and retention issues confronting women are not identical to those associated with minorities, although there are some over-riding issues; see, for instance, Rayman, 1991). While precollege efforts for minority students often focus on development of skills and experiences that can prepare them for further studies in science and/or engineering, the most common type of precollege program targeted at females was career fairs (N=5), followed by S&E summer programs (N=3). At the undergraduate level, engineering recruitment/retention programs were common program types for women

59

(N=5) as were S&E recruitment/retention programs (N=3) and student chapters of professional associations such as the Society of Women Engineers (N=3). There was only one identified effort targeted at women at the graduate level, an HCOP (Health Careers Opportunities Program). Three programs were identified as S&E faculty recruitment programs.[1] Based on this survey of a sizeable sample of undergraduate S&E programs, Matyas and Malcom conclude that the overall number of programs targeted at women is low; and at the precollege, graduate, and faculty levels, effective models are not necessarily the most likely to be implemented.

In general, programs targeted at women were more likely than were those for minority students to charge fees of program participants and to rely heavily on the use of faculty volunteers. Programs targeted at women do not generally include many minority women. Programs for minority students generally do a good job of recruiting black women into their programs, but Hispanic and Native American women were less likely to be participants (Matyas and Malcom, 1991).

In recent years, the number of women enrolling in engineering studies has been decreasing nationwide, and the efforts to recruit and retain them are becoming more sparse; notable exceptions are those engineering schools that offer merit awards for women and/or support student chapters of the Society of Women Engineers (Daniels, 1990). Data from a survey of women in engineering program directors indicated that the number and types of engineering program activities targeted toward women have significantly declined over the last decade (Daniels, 1990). With the exception of freshman scholarships and graduate fellowships, all types of program activities focused on the recruitment and retention of women in engineering declined nationally between 1982 and 1987. These activities included student chapters of the Society of Women Engineers, availability of recruitment brochures and information, programs for teachers and counselors, career conferences, summer programs, and junior high outreach activities (see Figure 4-3). This decline in program activities was paralleled or followed by a number of indicators suggesting that the absence of these activities may have affected the overall production of women engineers nationally:

- Between 1975 and 1982, the percentage of freshman women planning

---

[1] Six additional programs targeted at women were classified as "other."

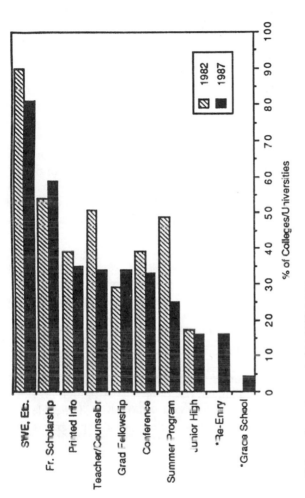

% of Colleges/Universities

*information not requested on 1982 survey

SOURCE: Jane Z. Daniels, A new W.E.P.A.N. for women in engineering, in S. Z. Keith and P. Keith, *Proceedings of the National Conference on Women in Mathematics and the Sciences*, St. Cloud, MN: St. Cloud State University, p. 222.

Figure 4-3. Percentage of colleges/universities offering women in engineering programs, 1987.

to major in engineering increased from a little over 1 percent to over 3 percent. However, after 1983, the percentage began a gradual decline (Vetter, 1989, p. 21).

- The proportion of women selecting "engineer" as a probable career choice increased from 2.2 percent in 1978 to a maximum of 3.6 percent in 1982 but has been declining since (Vetter, 1989, p. 23).
- The number of female freshmen enrolled in engineering peaked in 1982 and began to decline subsequently (AAES, 1989).
- The number of bachelor's degrees awarded to women in engineering leveled off in 1985 and ultimately peaked in 1987 at a slightly higher plateau (NSB, 1991).

Although causality cannot be confirmed by these data, the decline in women's expressed interest, enrollment, and earned degrees in engineering does not precede the declines in program activities. Rather, these phenomena parallel each other. Therefore, the declines in program activities were not initially prompted by a lack of women to participate in them. Finally, the more recent data indicate that this "parallel" relationship is continuing. In the last few years, program activities for women in engineering have been increasing (Wadsworth, 1992) and, concomitantly, enrollments of freshman women in engineering increased slightly in fall 1990 and more in fall 1991 to reach a record high of 17.5 percent (Vetter, 1992). Therefore, it appears that, in order to catalyze progressive increases in the number of women in engineering, continued intervention is needed.

In summary, few undergraduate S&E programs are today directed at the recruitment and retention of women, and the most effectively targeted models are not necessarily the most likely to be employed. Although previous work has provided a number of excellent program models that include the components of successful interventions, few of these model programs are targeted specifically at women.

Future Directions

The conference discussions as well as a number of recent reports (see, for instance, Clewell and Anderson, 1991; George, 1991; and White House Task Force, 1989) suggest a number of future steps for increasing the participation of women in science and engineering at the undergraduate level:

1   Higher education institutions should carefully monitor student progress to assess where "losses" of S&E students, especially women and minorities, occur and then define specific goals and strategies for increasing the participation of women in science and engineering.

2   Specific funding should be provided for S&E intervention programs targeted at women, particularly minority women. Relatively few funding agencies and foundations have funds set aside to specifically target undergraduate women. These new programs could be similar to those now in place for minorities underrepresented in the sciences and engineering.

3   Comprehensive intervention models should be targeted toward women and implemented in diverse institutions, particularly in those fields where the number of female undergraduate students is small compared to that of their male peers. These models should draw from effective programs already in place.

4   The research base on interventions for women in science and engineering at the undergraduate level should be expanded by funding longitudinal evaluations of selected programs.

5   New models should be developed, evaluated, revised, and disseminated for involving faculty members in strategies to increase the participation of undergraduate women in science and engineering. Both male and female faculty members must be involved in these efforts, and their participation should be viewed positively in terms of promotion and tenure review.

REFERENCES

American Association of Engineering Societies (AAES). 1989. Women in engineering. *Engineering Manpower Bulletin* 99:1-5.

Bird, Stephanie J. 1991. *Retaining Women Science Students: A Mentoring Project of the Association for Women in Science.* Paper presented at the National Research Council conference, "Science and Engineering Programs: On Target for Women?," Irvine, CA, November 4-5.

Brainard, Suzanne. 1991. *Mentoring Programs: Using a Generic Intervention Strategy.* Paper presented at the National Research Council conference on "Science and Engineering Programs: On Target for Women?," Irvine, CA, November 4-5.

Clewell, Beatriz C., and Bernice Anderson. 1991. *Women of Color in Mathematics, Science & Engineering.* Washington, DC: Center for Women Policy Studies.

Clewell, Beatriz C., and M. S. Ficklen. 1986. *Improving Minority Retention in Higher Education: A Search for Effective Institutional Practices* (Report No. RR-86-17). Princeton, NJ: Educational Testing Service.

Crovello, Theodore J. 1991. *Programs That Work: The Cal State-Los Angeles Experience and a General Campus Model.* Paper presented at the National Research Council conference, "Science and Engineering Programs: On Target for Women?," Irvine, CA, November 4-5.

Daniels, Jane Z. 1990. A new W.E.P.A.N. for women in engineering. In S. Z. Keith and P. Keith, *Proceedings of the National Conference on Women in Mathematics and the Sciences.* St. Cloud, MN: St. Cloud State University, pp. 217-222.

Garrison, Howard H., and Prudence W. Brown. 1985. *Minority Access to Research Careers: An Evaluation of the Honors Undergraduate Research Training Program.* Washington, DC: National Academy Press.

George, Yolanda S. 1991. Nurturing talent: Reports from the field. In Matyas and Malcom, 1991, *op cit.,* p. 127.

_____, Beatriz C. Chu-Clewell, and N. Watkins. 1987. *Lessons for HBCU's from Precollege Mathematics and Science Programs.* Paper commissioned by the White House Initiative on Historically Black Colleges and Universities for the symposium, "Alliances: An Expanded View," Washington, DC.

Hewitt, Nancy M., and Elaine Seymour. 1991. *Factors Contributing to High Attrition Rates Among Science, Mathematics, and Engineering Undergraduate Majors.* Boulder, CO: University of Colorado.

Malcom, Shirley M. 1983. *Equity and Excellence: Compatible Goals.* Washington, DC: American Association for the Advancement of Science.

Matyas, Marsha Lakes. 1987. Keeping undergraduate women in science and engineering: Contributing factors and recommendations for action. In J. Z. Daniels and J. B. Kahle. *Contributions to the Fourth GASAT Conference,* Volume 3. West Lafayette, IN: Purdue University Department of Freshman Engineering, pp. 112-122.

_____. 1988. *Intervention Programs in Mathematics and Science for Precollege Females: Program Types and Characteristics.* Invited research report and presentation for the Bush Foundation Board of Directors, St. Paul, MN.

_____, and Shirley M. Malcom. 1991. *Investing in Human Potential: Science and Engineering at the Crossroads.* Washington, DC: American Association for the Advancement of Science.

McCaffrey, Jacqueline P. 1991. *The Emerging Scholars Program at the University of Texas-Austin.* Paper presented at the National Research Council conference, "Science and Engineering Programs: On Target for Women?," Irvine, CA, November 4-5.

Muller, Carol B. 1991. Women in science: Changing attitudes and outcomes. *Directions* 6(1):2-5.

National Science Board (NSB). 1991. *Science and Engineering Indicators—1991.* Washington, DC: National Science Foundation.

Rayman, Paula. 1991. *Opportunities for Women in Science: The Undergraduate Experience.* Paper presented at the National Research Council conference, "Science and Engineering Programs: On Target for Women?," Irvine, CA, November 4-5.

Vetter, Betty M. 1992. *Professional Women and Minorities: A Total Human Resource Data Compendium.* Washington, DC: Commission on Professionals in Science and Technology.

_____. 1989. *Professional Women and Minorities.* Washington, DC: Commission on Professionals in Science and Technology.

Wadsworth, E. M. 1992. *Women in Engineering Program Advocates Network 1991 National Survey Frequencies.* West Lafayette, IN: Purdue University.

Wheeler, David L. 1992. Teaching calculus to minority students helps them stay in college. *The Chronicle of Higher Education* XXXVIII(41):A15, June 17.

White House Task Force on Women, Minorities, and the Handicapped in Science and Technology. 1989. *Changing America: The New Face of Science and Technology* (Final Report). Washington, DC: The Task Force.

Precise measurements of absorbed radiation dose for industrial and medical applications can be made at the NIST Electron Paramagnetic Resonance Facility. Here, physical science trainee Francoise Le inserts a bone fragment into the sample chamber.
(Photo: H. Mark Helfer, National Institute of Standards and Technology)

5

PROMOTING GRADUATE AND POSTDOCTORAL
STUDIES IN SCIENCE AND ENGINEERING

Joan Sherry
Linda Skidmore Dix

Joan Sherry is a free-lance science writer and editor who works in Chevy Chase, Maryland. Linda Skidmore Dix is the study director for the National Research Council's Committee on Women in Science and Engineering (CWSE). They developed this chapter from the formal presentations and discussions at the conference, "Science and Engineering Programs: On Target for Women?," held by CWSE at the Beckman Center, Irvine, CA, November 4-5, 1991.

Introduction

The graduate level is the bridge between interest and careers in science and engineering, but the percentage of U.S. students pursuing graduate degrees has begun to decline. Thus, interventions at this level are necessary not only to bring U.S. students into the field, but also to shape their view of themselves, their studies, and their professional colleagues. Graduate- and postdoctoral-level interventions aid the process whereby individuals form the networks that lead to job opportunities, shared research and, ultimately, a sense of the possibilities, both personal and professional, in their chosen fields of study. As shown in Figure 5-1, the percentage of women enrolled in graduate S&E programs is on the rise in all fields except computer science and the social sciences. Of some concern, however, is the lengthening time-to-degree of students pursuing doctorates in science and engineering. In all fields except engineering, women tend to have longer registered time-to-degree (RTD) and total time-to-degree (TTD), which is the total number of years elapsed between earning the baccalaureate and the doctorate, including time not enrolled at a university (Table 5-1). However, in most fields these differences are becoming minimal.

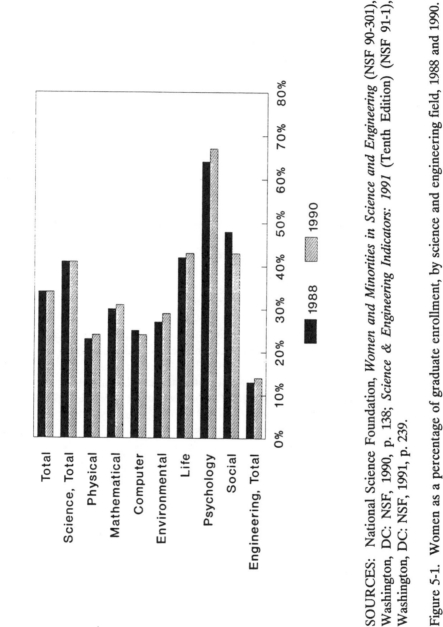

SOURCES: National Science Foundation, *Women and Minorities in Science and Engineering* (NSF 90-301), Washington, DC: NSF, 1990, p. 138; *Science & Engineering Indicators: 1991* (Tenth Edition) (NSF 91-1), Washington, DC: NSF, 1991, p. 239.

Figure 5-1. Women as a percentage of graduate enrollment, by science and engineering field, 1988 and 1990.

TABLE 5-1: Median Years to Degree for Doctorate Recipients, by Demographic Group and Broad Field, 1990

	All Fields	Physical Sci.*	Engineering	Life Sci.	Social Sci	Humanities	Education	Prof/Other
RTD Years								
All Ph.D.s	7.0	6.2	6.0	6.7	7.5	8.3	8.1	7.5
Men	6.7	6.2	6.0	6.6	7.4	8.3	8.0	7.3
Women	7.4	6.3	6.1	6.8	7.7	8.3	8.1	7.5
U.S. Citizens	7.2	6.2	6.0	6.7	7.7	8.4	8.3	7.7
Permanent Res.	7.1	6.7	6.5	6.7	7.8	8.5	7.5	7.3
Temporary Res.	6.3	6.3	6.0	6.5	6.9	7.4	6.1	6.3
TTD Years								
All Ph.D.s	10.5	7.6	8.2	9.1	10.6	12.2	17.9	13.1
Men	9.6	7.6	8.2	8.8	10.4	11.9	17.3	12.3
Women	12.6	7.6	7.8	9.7	10.8	12.5	18.4	14.9
U.S. Citizens	11.4	7.2	7.8	9.0	10.9	12.5	18.4	14.4
Permanent Res.	9.8	8.7	8.6	9.5	10.4	11.1	13.6	11.0
Temporary Res.	8.9	8.1	8.3	9.3	9.5	10.2	12.8	10.3

NOTE: Medians are based on the number of individuals who have provided complete information about their postbaccalaureate education. See technical notes in Appendix C for rates of nonresponse to the applicable questions.

*Includes mathematics and computer sciences.

SOURCE: Delores H. Thurgood and Joanne M. Weinman, *Summary Report 1990: Doctorate Recipients from United States Universities,* Washington, DC: National Academy Press, 1991.

Experience indicates that successful programs at the graduate level of education are addressed to specifically identified needs, demonstrate multiple linkages between graduate school and other populations, and are characterized by substantial faculty or mentor commitment. This chapter discusses some model graduate and postdoctoral interventions sponsored by professional societies, universities, private foundations and companies, and federal agencies. The Irvine conference presentations significantly broadened the definition of intervention at the graduate level by suggesting a wide spectrum of programs and outcomes aimed at recruitment and retention of women in S&E (Marrett, 1991). While many of the interventions discussed involve financial aid programs, others go beyond. The spectrum includes:

- studies of the patterns of participation by women in all activities at the graduate level. The processes by which men and women move through graduate school activities are not necessarily the same; do we know in what ways they are different?
- initiatives and efforts that are not interventions in a structural sense but nevertheless affect outcomes—for example, student membership in professional societies, caucuses, associations, support groups, and coalitions. Such associations provide intangible as well as tangible benefits and often benefit older, professional members of the group as much as students.
- systemic approaches that alter institutions or settings. A teaching fellowship training program that includes training on sensitivity to gender issues is an intervention that can change the setting in which teaching and research are done and in which the pursuit of careers takes place.
- grassroots efforts. All effective programs are not necessarily created centrally and may benefit the creators as much or more than the populations at whom they are directed.

Interventions Sponsored by Professional Societies

Professional societies make a valuable and positive contribution to the promotion of women in science and engineering. According to Kagiwada (1991), such societies provide proof that women scientists and engineers do exist and offer a forum for recognizing outstanding performance by women professionals in S&E fields; serve as points of contact for women who wish to interact with others in their specific disciplines or in science and engineering in general; provide financial aid to undergraduate and graduate students as well as to postdoctoral women who need a boost to continue their work and their careers; offer career advancement training seminars and workshops as well as technical seminars for the presentation of research papers; offer opportunities for leadership and the development of managerial and administrative skills through volunteer participation in the society's organization and work; and offer friendship and camaraderie with fellow members, thus forming a network that cuts across many traditional boundaries.

Graduate Women in Science (GWIS) is an example of such a professional society. It was founded by a group of graduate women students at Cornell in 1921 as a scientific fraternity for women. Membership requires a degree in science or engineering and research or equivalent professional experience. The society has provided financial aid from its earliest days, when members collected and distributed $50 to members needing money for research. Currently, potential award recipients are identified from responses to an annual advertisement in *Science* magazine. The total annual amount of the awards is derived from endowments made from the estates of members. In the 1990-91 fiscal year, 270 applications were received and 7 awards made, totaling $20,000 (Kagiwada, 1991).[1]

At the graduate level, the need for mentoring continues with an increased focus on career advice and professional goals. The structure of the graduate mentoring program sponsored by the Association for Women in Science, with funding from the Alfred P. Sloan Foundation, remains very similar to the format of its undergraduate program (see Chapter 4). Chapter activities facilitate communication and support among women at all levels who are interested in science, as well as provide mechanisms for women science professionals to share their experience and understanding of the social structure and function of the scientific community with students. An emphasis on career-directing occurs with discussions on career paths, balancing a career and family, dual career families as well as greater exposure to the scientific

---

[1] In addition to the graduate level aid, several local chapters provide undergraduate scholarships by soliciting donations from local companies. The association also presents recognition awards to outstanding women in science and engineering.

71

community through attendance at professional meetings and development of colleagues beyond the institution in which the mentoring program is based.

Other programs sponsored by professional societies are listed in Appendix A. Although most of the programs do not specifically target women, they nevertheless have provided assistance to women.

Interventions Sponsored by Universities

Linkage or interaction at all levels—graduate and undergraduate student bodies, administration, and faculty—was a recurring theme in both the conference presentations and deliberations of successful interventions at the graduate and postdoctoral levels (see, for instance, Sheridan, 1991) and is evident in many of the programs listed in Appendix A. Another recurring theme was the need to identify issues before taking action (Marrett, 1991).

There are many ways to achieve linkages. The programs described below demonstrate three kinds of linkages:

- administrative/functional, through centralized management of fellowships, access programs, and faculty and teaching assistant (TA) training;
- institutional, through creation of structures within the university that encourage the interaction of populations and levels; and
- consortial, through programs implemented at numerous institutional sites and coordinated by an external organization.

A clarification of each of these types of linkages is provided by the illustrative examples given in the text below.

Administrative Linkages

The University of Missouri-Columbia competitive fellowship program for minorities, the Gus T. Ridgel program, initiated in 1989 and targeted mainly but not exclusively toward African-Americans, illustrates administrative linkage. The program provides two-year support for master's students and four-year support for Ph.D. candidates. The $12,000 annual stipend comes from $9,000 in centralized university funds and $3,000 in departmental research or teaching assistantship funds. The commitment of departmental funds encourages faculty participation and helps to assure that minority

72

recipients participate in departmental activities as much as other research (RAs) or teaching assistants (TAs) (Sheridan, 1991). Of the 70 African-American students in the program thus far, 20 are in science and engineering, and 9 of them are women. The program is managed through a single Office of Fellowships and Graduate Student Affairs under an Associate Dean, with responsibility for recruitment of all graduate students, not just minorities. That office also administers the university's graduate access programs. Training of TAs and training and support for excellence in teaching by faculty at Missouri-Columbia are also administered by a single university office, that of the Vice Provost for Minority Affairs and Faculty Development. A number of federal grant programs at the university are both obtained and administered by the same support office, even though the programs may be in different departments.

The present TA training program at Missouri-Columbia includes an intervention that has affected the institutional setting for graduate education. The training program at the university was organized in response to a law passed by the Missouri legislature requiring specialized training or a special exemption for TAs whose native language was not English. The university set up a special program that quickly evolved to a program including most of the American TAs, as well as the foreign-born assistants. The program has been so successful that, over a three-year period, student and parent complaints dropped from repeated to essentially no complaints (Sheridan, 1991). One of the more successful elements in the program, and one that changed gender sensitivity attitudes, has been the videotaping with feedback sessions that are part of the training course. Although the trainers originally assumed gender sensitivity would be more of a problem for foreign trainees than for Americans, this did not turn out to be the case. It was rather a problem of individuals, American as well as foreign, many of whom did not realize what they were doing when addressing women students until they saw themselves on tape. The videotape sessions are now included in training for new faculty, as well as for TAs.

Institutional Linkages

Another example of linkage at Missouri-Columbia is the Graduate Outreach Workshop (G.R.O.W.). The objectives of this student-initiated and student-run program include the following:

> to interest all students, especially women and minorities, in
> science and science careers; to illustrate basic principles of

research with real-life examples of graduate research; and to decrease student anxiety about science and science fields (Sheridan, 1991).

The program is directed at junior and senior high school students, and Dean Sheridan reports it started in reaction to an article written by Carl Sagan lamenting the problem of scientific literacy and the decreasing number of younger students going into science. The graduate students said, "You know, what we are doing is exciting; how come kids in junior high school and high school don't understand it? Maybe we can do something about it." They wrote to a number of high school teachers but received no response. Rather than be dissuaded, the students organized themselves in order to go through the process of obtaining a $2,000 Kellogg grant through the university's extension division. By late 1991, G.R.O.W. had made five presentations and had six more scheduled, all on the original $2,000 grant. A high proportion of the participants are women. There are 20 active G.R.O.W. students, of whom 13 are women, and more are being recruited (by G.R.O.W. students) from several departments in the biomedical sciences.

The importance of the G.R.O.W. example lies as much, or perhaps more, in its effect on the graduate student initiators as on the secondary school students at whom the program is aimed. The example of graduate students endeavoring to communicate to others their own excitement about science while still in graduate school bodes well for the future of the professoriate as well as for research. Furthermore, that concept is endorsed by both students and faculty. For instance, at the Presidential Young Investigator (PYI) Colloquium on U.S. Engineering, Mathematics, and Science Education for the Year 2010 and Beyond, held on November 4-6, 1990, participants noted that:

> Students must be active contributors in their own education and in the education of their fellow students. . . . Prerequisites should not necessarily impede a student's progress; for example, we suggest student tutoring teams be formed in classes with prerequisites in which students will help fellow team members with prerequisite material they know best, and vice versa (NSF, 1992).

Furthermore, the PYIs recommended that higher education

74

develop prestigious teaching internships for engineering, mathematics, and science graduate students aspiring to faculty careers in higher education. The internships would be to recruit and better prepare graduate students for their full responsibilities as future members of academe, and especially to improve their abilities in effective teaching and instructional scholarship (NSF, 1992).

Another institutional linkage program is the University of Maryland's program in toxicology. At that university, retention rather than recruitment of graduate students in the field of toxicology was identified as the real need. To enhance retention, Fowler (1991) points out there must be an environment that permits students to develop confidence in themselves and their work, substantial commitment on the part of faculty, and money to fund the interventions.

The Maryland program, which included 20 women and 10 men in 1991, establishes a confidence-building environment by inviting student-run seminars and including student evaluations of the seminars; encouraging student participation in scientific meetings; and bringing in a series of outside speakers who act as role models or mentors. Another important feature is an open management style that gives the students access to the program director in his/her office at any time. The program gives students up to two years to select an adviser and includes rotating laboratory assignments with faculty during this initial period.

Faculty interest and funding are both aided by the program's focus on multidisciplinary research projects. Grants for multidisciplinary investigations are often easier to obtain than those for narrower projects, but the key factor, according to Director Fowler, is diversity of funding sources, since nothing works all the time.

Even though the program has been overwhelmingly successful, certain problems have not been overcome—for example, self-limiting behavior by students because of prior life experience and funding cutbacks by the state because of unfavorable economic conditions. The program has been evaluated by the NIH Training Grant Review process and the University of Maryland self-study review.

A third example of institutional linkage can be found at the University of California at Berkeley. From 1985 to 1990, women at Berkeley earned

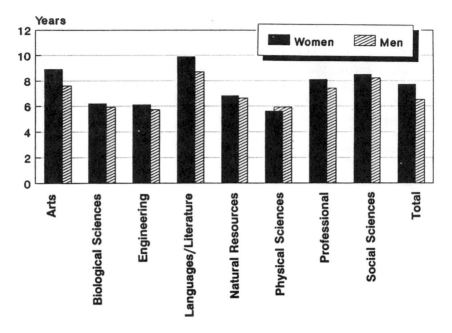

SOURCE: Maresi Nerad, *Using Time, Money, and Human Resources Efficiently and Effectively in the Case of Women Graduate Students*, paper prepared for conference on "Science and Engineering Programs: On Target for Women?," Irvine, CA, November 4-5, 1991.

Figure 5-2. Mean time to doctoral degree, University of California-Berkeley, 1986-1991, by sex.

approximately half of all undergraduate degrees but only 30 percent of all graduate degrees. In many fields, there is a 50 percent reduction in women's participation rate from undergraduate to graduate studies (Nerad, 1991). In light of these statistics and the need to identify the specific situations that give rise to them, the Graduate Research section of the Graduate Division at Berkeley has begun systematic and continuous analysis of graduate admissions and programs and has institutionalized programs through which faculty, students, and graduate department secretaries can apply the results of the Graduate Division's data collection and analyses. These programs are discussed in greater detail below.

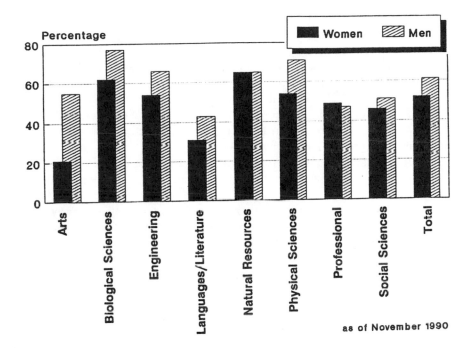

Percentage

■ Women ▨ Men

as of November 1990

SOURCE: Maresi Nerad, *Using Time, Money, and Human Resources Efficiently and Effectively in the Case of Women Graduate Students*, paper prepared for conference on "Science and Engineering Programs: On Target for Women?," Irvine, CA, November 4-5, 1991.

Figure 5-3. Doctoral completion rates, University of California-Berkeley, 1978-79 cohort, by sex.

Berkeley's analysis of institutional data revealed the following:

• The average time-to-degree for all doctoral recipients (3,917) from 1986-1991 was 6.5 years, with the average time for women 7.7 years. However, women took slightly less time than men in the physical sciences (5.6 versus 5.9 years), and only slightly longer than men in the biological sciences (6.2 versus 5.9 years) and engineering (6.1 versus 5.7 years) (see Figure 5-2).

77

- In science and engineering Ph.D. programs, the completion rates of women were about 15 percent lower than those of men. Women were found to have a higher attrition rate than men both before and after advancement to candidacy, with the exception of the biological sciences (see Figure 5-3).
- However, if all kinds of financial support, particularly RAs, are distributed equally between men and women and if campus child-care is provided, then women tend to finish the doctorate as quickly as men do (Nerad and Cerny, 1991).
- A higher proportion of women were dissatisfied with the departmental advising and the professional help they received from their dissertation adviser. In the biological sciences, 21 percent of the women were dissatisfied versus 9 percent of the men; in physical sciences, 15 percent versus 10 percent; and in engineering, 12 percent versus 8 percent. There appear to be at least three explanations for women's greater dissatisfaction: (a) faculty behave differently toward women and men; (b) faculty behave similarly to women and men but the two sexes interpret the behavior differently; and (c) women suffer more in the "chilly" departmental climate than men do.[2]

Nerad reports that the absence of positive feedback seems to affect women and men students differently. An "I don't have any real problems with it" reaction from faculty tends to be interpreted by women as "What did I do wrong? What could I have done better?" Men tend to accept the comment as, "Go ahead! You're doing fine." Women students begin doubting their intellectual capability and tend to become demoralized; men may be disappointed but remain sure of their intellectual capacity. These differential interpretations may result from the tendency of women to apply the same set of rules to faculty as they might apply to themselves in a similar situation. Nerad gives an example of a graduate woman TA's reaction to two Biology 1 undergraduate students:

> If I have a Biology 1 student who writes a lousy paper, I couldn't imagine not saying, "You have some very good ideas

---

[2]Bernice Sandler coined this term. See publications of the Project on the Status and Education of Women, Association of American Colleges, 1982, 1984, 1986.

here, but let's think about your organization." On the other end of the scale is the Biology 1 student who writes a really good paper, and the TA hands it back, saying, "Well, Fred, I don't have any major problems with this."

This TA could not imagine giving such feedback to her student.

The departmental climate also affects women differently. Women students at Berkeley tend to believe that lack of departmental attention and caring means they don't deserve to keep going or that they must not be good enough. Most male doctoral students, conversely, are more self-confident and consider themselves entitled to an advanced degree, so the absence of departmental caring does not seem to bother them as much as it does women.

Berkeley accepts the premise that departmental climate and culture play an important part in the progress of doctoral students, particularly women and minorities. To improve this climate and reduce overall attrition rates in graduate school, the Graduate Division at Berkeley has institutionalized a number of programs that bring together the faculty, students, and departmental graduate secretaries. This approach includes:

- data collection through studies of the graduate school population, including recruitment, retention, and performance indicators (data are disaggregated by sex, ethnicity, and field of study at each stage of the doctoral program);
- questionnaire surveys of doctoral students at the time dissertations are filed, eliciting their views on how their needs have been met by departments, faculty, and advisers (the results are summarized and sent to departments with a letter from the Dean pointing out positive developments and asking for responses to students' comments on their level of satisfaction with the department);
- monthly student focus groups, usually made up of one or two students selected from each department in a major field of study each semester, that discuss the students' concerns regarding their programs and the Division's research findings and suggest programmatic activities;
- development of a guide to the kinds of help available to students during the various stages of the doctoral program;
- monthly faculty invitational seminars as a forum to develop policy (a different group of faculty is selected each semester);

- a Graduate Division requirement that every student meet with two or three faculty members at least once a year to discuss his or her past year's accomplishments and projected following year program in order to get feedback; and
- visits by the graduate dean to five or six departments each semester to talk separately with faculty, students, and affirmative action advisers (visits are preceded by a letter or other material suggesting issues that might be on the agenda).

By focusing on the different stages of a doctoral program, on specific needs of the student during these stages, and on the departmental learning climate, the Berkeley approach seems to have been particularly helpful to women (Nerad, 1991).

Consortial Linkages

An example of such an intervention to retain scientists and engineers in graduate study is the GEM Engineering/Science Fellowship Program, established in 1976 by the National Consortium for Graduate Degrees for Minorities in Engineering and Science, Inc. (GEM). Each year, GEM awards fellowships to American Indian, black American, Mexican American, and Puerto Rican students pursuing master's degrees in engineering and Ph.D.s in either science or engineering. Master's degree students are expected to complete their degrees in no more than three semesters or four quarters, while length of awards to Ph.D. students varies with the S&E discipline and university requirements. The overall graduation rate for participants in this program has been 86 percent since its inception.

None of the GEM programs operate independently. Rather, sponsorship is broad, with coordination handled by the offices in Notre Dame, Indiana. The GEM M.S. in Engineering Program is sponsored by 62 university members and 77 research laboratory members. The GEM Ph.D. in Engineering Program is sponsored by 53 university members; and 41 universities and 14 research laboratories sponsor the GEM Ph.D. in Science Program. Among the participating universities are the following: Georgia Institute of Technology, Hampton University (Virginia), Howard University (Washington, DC), Massachusetts Institute of Technology, Morgan State University (Maryland), New Mexico State University, North Carolina A&T State University, Prairie View A&M University, Southern University (Louisiana), Stanford University (California), Tuskegee University, University of California-Los Angeles, University of Michigan, University of Puerto Rico-

TABLE 5-2: Numbers of Students Holding GEM Fellowships, 1991

GEM Program	Race/Ethnicity and Sex								Total	
	American Indian		Black American		Mexican American		Puerto Rican			
	M	F	M	F	M	F	M	F	M	F
M.S., Engineering	5	1	95	70	31	6	12	6	143	83
Ph.D., Engineering	1	1	11	5	2	2	3	2	17	10
Ph.D., Science	0	1	6	19	1	4	1	0	8	24
Total Numbers	6	3	112	94	34	12	16	8	168	117

SOURCE: Data from the National Consortium for Graduate Degrees for Minorities in Engineering and Science, Inc., 1992.

Mayaguez, University of Tennessee, and University of Texas-El Paso. Table 5-2 gives the profile of students holding GEM fellowships in 1991.

Interventions Sponsored by the Private Sector

Numerous private organizations support programs that encourage U.S. students to pursue advanced education and careers in the sciences and engineering. Highlighted below are some programs supported by the Ford Foundation, Howard Hughes Medical Institute, and Alfred P. Sloan Foundation as well as others in the private sector.

Ford Foundation

The Ford Foundation sponsors two programs administered by the National Research Council's Office of Scientific and Engineering Personnel (OSEP): (1) Predoctoral and Dissertation Fellowships for Minorities and (2) Postdoctoral Fellowships for Minorities. In both programs, fellowships are offered on a competitive basis to individuals who are citizens or nationals of the United States and members of the following groups: Alaskan Natives

TABLE 5-3: Participation in the Ford Foundation Predoctoral and Dissertation Fellowships for Minorities Program, FY 1992, by Sex

	Applications			Awards		
	M	F	T	M	F	T
Biological Sciences	73	93 (56%)	166	6	4 (40%)	10
Engineering, Mathematics, & Physical Sciences	186	134 (41.9%)	320	16	1 (5.9%)	17
Behavioral & Social Sciences Psychology	43	172 (80%)	215	2	10 (83.3%)	12
Social Sciences	129	189 (59.4%)	318	5	13 (72.2%)	18
Total, Behavioral & Social	172	361 (67.7%)	533	7	23 (76.7%)	30
TOTAL, ALL FIELDS	431	588 (57.7%)	1,019	29	28 (49.1%)	57

SOURCE: National Research Council, Office of Scientific and Engineering Personnel, Fellowship Office.

(Eskimo or Aleut), black/African Americans, Mexican Americans/Chicanos, Native American Indians, Native Pacific Islanders (Polynesian or Micronesian), and Puerto Ricans. The goals of the programs are to identify individuals of demonstrated ability who are members of these minority groups traditionally underrepresented in the behavioral and social sciences, engineering, mathematics, physical sciences, and life sciences and to encourage awardees "to achieve their full potential as scholars who will inspire others to follow an academic career in teaching and research" (1992 program announcement). As shown in Tables 5-3 and 5-4, in general, greater numbers

TABLE 5-4: Participation in the Ford Postdoctoral Fellowships for Minorities Program, FY 1992, by Sex

	Applicants			Awards		
	M	F	T	M	F	T
Biological Sciences	11	6 (35.3%)	17	4	1 (20%)	5
Physical Sciences, Mathematics & Engineering	6	4 (40%)	10	2	1 (33.3%)	3
Psychology	3	4 (57.1%)	7	1	1 (50%)	2
Social Sciences	7	17 (70.8%)	24	1	5 (20%)	6
TOTAL, ALL FIELDS	41	49 (54.4%)	90	12	13 (52%)	25

SOURCE: National Research Council, Office of Scientific and Engineering Personnel, Fellowship Office.

of women than men apply for Ford Fellowships, but women receive about half of the total awards. As in similar programs, the distribution by specific fields varies. In addition, the percentage of awards to women more closely parallels their percentage of applicants in the postdoctoral program than in the predoctoral/dissertation fellowship program.

Howard Hughes Medical Institute (HHMI)
HHMI, a nonprofit "philanthropic organization dedicated to basic biomedical research and education" (1992 program announcement), sponsors a program of financial support for graduate work in research-based doctoral programs (Ph.D. or Sc.D) in the biological sciences—specifically, biochemistry, biophysics, biostatistics, cell biology and regulation, develop-

TABLE 5-5: Participation, by Sex, in the Howard Hughes Medical Institute Predoctoral Fellowship Program in the Biological Sciences, FY 1988-1992

		Applicants		Awards	
		No.	%	No.	%
FY 1992	Female	697	50.0	35	50.0
	Male	696	50.0	35	50.0
FY 1991	Female	719	50.2	25	36.2
	Male	713	49.8	44	63.7
FY 1990	Female	586	49.1	28	41.2
	Male	608	50.9	40	58.8
FY 1989	Female	520	49.8	19	31.1
	Male	524	50.2	42	68.9
FY 1988	Female	506	46.6	20	33.3
	Male	580	53.4	40	66.7

SOURCE: National Research Council, Office of Scientific and Engineering Personnel, Fellowship Office.

mental biology, epidemiology, genetics, immunology, mathematical biology, microbiology, molecular biology, neuroscience, pharmacology, physiology, structural biology, and virology. The goals of the HHMI Predoctoral Fellowships in Biological Sciences, launched in 1987, are "the advancement of fundamental knowledge in the biomedical sciences and the application of new scientific knowledge to the alleviation of disease and the promotion of health." For the first time, in 1992, the program achieved gender parity in the awarding of fellowships to women and men (Table 5-5), while in its earlier years, men had a much greater likelihood of success.

Alfred P. Sloan Foundation

The Sloan Foundation for some time has supported programs to enhance women's education and to improve science and engineering education in general. The Sloan Foundation gives money for intervention implementation as well as for model studies. Program support can be quite long-term for foundations, but it does not go on indefinitely. Two programs dealing with general graduate education and currently supported by this Foundation are found at Arizona State University (ASU) and Cornell University. ASU's Project 1000 is "a cooperative effort among 72 selective public and private comprehensive doctoral-granting institutions, over 155 colleges and universities with significant U.S. Hispanic undergraduate enrollment, concerned corporations, and various related national and community-based Hispanic organizations" (Sloan, 1991). Begun in 1991, its performance goals are to increase the number of U.S. Hispanic students *applying* and *admitted* to graduate school in mathematics, the physical sciences, engineering, and technology-related fields. A study, "Econometric Estimation of Doctoral Student Time-to-Degree and Completion Probability Models," is being undertaken by Professor Ronald G. Ehrenberg in Cornell University's School of Industrial and Labor Relations. A major aim of the study is to determine how different variables influence non-completion rates of graduate students and to "provide evidence on how improved support for graduate students and improved job market conditions would likely affect doctoral students' time-to-degree and completion rates in the future" (Sloan, 1991). Although both of these activities focus on broad groups—U.S. Hispanic graduate students in the first case and all graduate students in the second example—the descriptive literature does not specify efforts that focus on women. One Sloan-supported initiative that does focus on women is the mentoring project of the Association for Women in Science, which attempts to recruit and retain both highly capable undergraduates and graduate students in scientific careers (see Chapter 4). According to Stephanie Bird, former AWIS president, "The AWIS Mentoring Project focuses on graduate students as much as it does undergraduates" (Bird, 1992).

Private Corporations

Similarly, a number of private corporations, as well as many of the privately-funded national laboratories, provide scholarships, fellowships, and temporary employment programs aimed at identifying and developing potential scientists and engineers. Some of these are targeted to women and minorities (see Appendix Tables A-2 through A-6). Corporate sponsorship is provided either by the firm individually, or as part of a consortium such as the National Physical Science Consortium. Among programs sponsored by individual firms and specifically targeted to women are American Telephone

85

& Telegraph (AT&T) Company's Graduate Research Program for Women, the Summer Research Program for Minorities and Women, and the Summer University Relations Program; Hewlett-Packard's Student Employment and Education Development (SEED) Internship; and the Bristol-Myers-Squibb Clairol Mentor Program.

An example of a jointly sponsored program targeted at women and minorities is the National Physical Science Consortium (NPSC), which links more than 68 graduate institutions and 27 employers (Snow, 1991). Corporate employers provide six-year fellowships in astronomy, physics, chemistry, material science, mathematics, geology, and computer science. The universities provide full tuition and admission fees. Sponsoring organizations provide two summers of employment for meaningful research at their laboratories, as well as mentors, overhead support, and money for student stipends. Recipients must be U.S. citizens and can be undergraduate seniors, master's candidates at non-Ph.D.-granting universities, or returning students who have been in industry for more than a year. A minimum 3.0 GPA (of a possible 4.0 GPA) is required, and the average awardee has a 3.6. Thus far, the consortium has received the most employer support for fellowships in physics and the least in chemistry and materials science.

The consortium began with a goal to increase the number of minority and female Ph.D.s in the physical sciences; the organizational process to achieve this goal was developed by a local task force organized at Lawrence Livermore National Laboratory. The local task force eventually became a national task force and then the first board of directors for the consortium. The administrative center for the consortium is at the University of California-San Diego in La Jolla. New Mexico State University, because it is a center for American Indian and Hispanic populations in the Southwest and West, is the focus area for student recruitment.

Recruitment is carried out primarily through personal contact by staff and referrals from professors and other students. About 60 percent of the applicants have been white females; the rest are minorities including black females. Awards, on the other hand, have been about 57 percent to minority students and the rest to white and Asian females. Initial screening of applicants is carried out in December of each year by a committee from participating universities. In 1991 the committee came from 13 universities. The committee selects two candidate pools, a top applicant group (about 5 to 1 for each fellowship position) and a pool of those who survived the first cut-off but did not make the top list. A booklet with demographics of all selected applicants and copies of their applications, as well as certain computer configurations of applicants in the top pool, is sent to employers. The employers send representatives to La Jolla in January, and the selection is made by a method similar to that of a football draft—each employer takes a number out of a hat and when the number is drawn, picks the first student remaining in the pool who is on the employer's list. The diverse national distribution of employers and student applicants insures that each member employer gets their optimal choice from their list of top students. The student dropout rate for the consortium has been approximately 4 percent. In 1991 NSPC awarded 48 fellowships and they will award 85 in 1992.

Interventions Sponsored by Federal Agencies

Among the many graduate education programs sponsored by federal agencies are two administered within the National Research Council's Office of Scientific and Engineering Education for the National Science Foundation: the NSF Graduate Fellowship Program and the NSF Minority Graduate Fellowship Program.

National Science Foundation (NSF) Graduate Fellowship Program

The NSF Graduate Fellowship Program is open to U.S. citizens or nationals and permanent resident aliens of the United States for advanced study in the mathematical, physical, biological, engineering, and behavioral and social sciences, as well as in the history and philosophy of science. In addition to the annual awards dispersed across these disciplines, NSF allocates about 70 awards for Graduate Fellowships for Women in Engineering. As shown in Table 5-6, except in earth science, increasing numbers of students, both women and men, are applying for these fellowships. However, in most fields, the percentage of women receiving awards is almost always smaller than the percentage of women applying. In four areas—chemistry, applied mathematics and statistics, mathematics, and computer science—the disproportions are strikingly large.

NSF Minority Graduate Fellowship Program

The objective of this program, begun in 1978, is "to increase the number of scientists who are members of ethnic minority groups under-represented at the advanced levels of science, mathematics, and engineering" (NSF, 1988). The program is open to U.S. students who are members of the following ethnic groups—American Indian, Black American, Hispanic, Native

87

TABLE 5-6: NSF Graduate Fellowship Program Applications and Awards, by Sex, 1985 and 1992

Discipline	1985		1992		1985		1992	
	M	W	M	W	M	W	M	W
	Total Applicants				Total Awards			
N	2776	1614	4387	3336	362	178	450	290
%	63.2	36.8	56.8	43.2	67.0	33.0	60.8	39.2
Biochem*	246	167	268	268	32	16	26	23
	59.6	40.4	50.0	50.0	66.7	33.3	53.1	46.9
Biology	298	274	364	499	32	40	27	46
	52.1	42.9	42.2	57.8	44.4	55.6	37.0	63.0
Chemistry	219	118	293	160	32	9	39	8
	65.0	35.0	64.7	35.3	78.0	22.0	83.0	17.0
Earth Sci	151	88	125	87	20	9	12	7
	63.2	36.8	59.0	41.0	69.0	31.0	63.1	36.9
Appl Math/	80	39	106	89	14	1	13	3
Statistics	67.2	32.8	54.3	45.7	93.3	6.7	81.2	18.8
Mathematics	105	43	175	83	19	1	23	3
	70.9	29.1	67.8	32.2	95.0	5.0	88.5	11.5
Physics and	309	44	394	93	39	6	35	12
Astronomy	87.5	12.5	80.9	19.1	86.7	13.3	74.5	25.5
Behavioral	397	436	791	935	50	50	77	65
Sciences**	47.7	52.3	45.8	54.2	50.0	50.0	54.2	45.8
Biomedical	154	208	192	279	15	28	14	25
Sciences	42.5	57.5	40.8	59.2	42.5	57.5	35.9	64.1
Computer	182	54	302	90	27	3	30	2
Science	77.1	22.9	77.0	23.0	90.0	10.0	93.8	6.2
Engineering	635	143	1377	753	82	15	154	96
	81.6	18.4	64.7	35.3	84.5	15.5	61.6	38.4

* Includes biochemsitry, biophysics, and molecular biology.
**Prior to 1991, this field included psychology, economics, and sociology. Becasue the disaggregation of behavioral sciences—into (1) anthropology, sociology, and linguistics; (2) economicis, urban planning, and history of sciences; (3) political science, international relations, and geography; and (4) psychology—did not occur until 1991, a single category is used here.
SOURCE: National Resource Council, Office of Scientific and Engineering Personnel, Fellowships Office.

Alaskan, or Native Pacific Islander—for "if we genuinely want to achieve our goal of filling vacant faculty, research, and industrial positions, we will find ourselves increasingly dependent on minority talent" (Bloch, 1988). As shown in Table 5-7, gender equity in both applications and awards has, in the aggregate, been reached. However, disparities occur in broad fields—that is, greater percentages of women apply for awards in the biosciences and behavioral sciences while men tend to apply for fellowships in the physical sciences and engineering. It should also be noted that the success rate of women is much higher in the fields of chemistry, earth science, physics/astronomy/mathematics, and behavioral sciences in the Minority Graduate Program than in NSF's Graduate Fellowship Program.

Postdoctoral Research Associateship Program

Many federal programs provide an opportunity for individual scientists and engineers to link their own research projects to the ongoing work of federal research centers. One such program is the Research Associateships Program administered by the National Research Council (NRC), which provides support for one- to three-year periods for "postdoctoral scientists and engineers of unusual promise and ability." The program expects to award approximately 350 new Research Associateships in 1992, for a total of approximately $30 million. The NRC Postdoctoral Research Associateships (PRAs) are open to U.S. citizens (with one exception) who have completed doctorates within five years of the date of application. Resident Research Associateships are open to citizen and foreign national senior investigators as well as to recent doctoral graduates. Senior Research Associateships are open to applicants who have held a doctorate for more than five years. Appendix A lists programs offered in 1992. Figure 5-4 reveals the increasing number of PRAs awarded to women in recent years; the decline in numbers of awards to both women and men, beginning in 1990, reflects the fact that 1990 was the first year in which awardees could receive third-year funding for their research, limiting the number of new awards made by the laboratories. Drawing from Figure 5-4, we note that the percentage of PRAs awarded to women has more than doubled since 1979, although the progress has not been steady:

Year	% to Women	Year	% to Women	Year	% to Women
1979	8.9	1984	13.7	1988	21.0
1980	9.6	1985	18.4	1989	19.3
1981	12.0	1986	15.2	1990	18.6
1982	8.4	1987	20.4	1991	19.3

89

TABLE 5-7: NSF Minority Graduate Fellowship Program Applications and Awards, by Sex, 1985 and 1992

Discipline		1985		1992	
		Men	Women	Men	Women
Total Applicants	N	298	305	713	767
	%	49.4	50.6	48.2	51.8
Biosciences*		62	79	107	169
		44.0	56.0	38.8	61.2
Chemistry/Earth Science		27	22	46	54
		55.1	44.9	46.0	54.0
Physics/Astronomy/Math		37	32	114	92
		53.6	46.4	55.3	44.7
Behavioral Science**		68	116	183	287
		37.0	63.0	38.9	61.1
Engineering		65	35	263	165
		65.0	35.0	61.4	38.6
Total Awards	N	39	21	61	59
	%	65.0	35.0	50.8	49.2
Biosciences*		10	5	12	8
		66.7	33.3	60.0	40.0
Chemistry/ Earth Science		2	2	2	5
		50.0	50.0	28.6	71.4
Physics/Astronomy/ Math		6	1	7	8
		85.7	14.3	46.7	53.3
Behavioral Science**		12	11	13	22
		52.2	47.8	37.1	62.9
Engineering		9	2	27	16
		81.8	18.2	62.8	37.2

* Includes biology, biochemistry, biophysics, and biomedical science.
**Includes anthropology, sociology, and linguistics; economics, urban planning, and history of science; political science, international relations, and geography; and psychology.
SOURCE: National Research Council, Office of Scientific and Engineering Personnel, Fellowships Office.

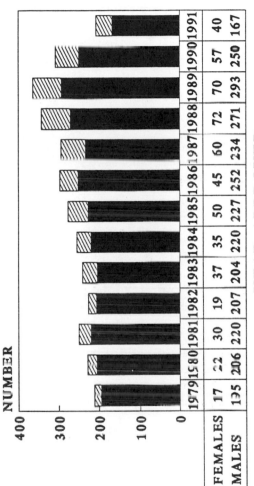

	1979	1980	1981	1982	1983	1984	1985	1986	1987	1988	1989	1990	1991
FEMALES	17	22	30	19	37	35	50	45	60	72	70	57	40
MALES	195	206	220	207	204	220	227	252	234	271	293	250	167

YEAR APPROVED

■ MALES ▨ FEMALES

SOURCE: National Research Council, Office of Scientific and Engineering Personnel, Committee on NRC Research Associates' Career Outcomes.

Figure 5-4. Number of new awards, NRC Postdoctoral Research Associateship Program, 1979-1991, by sex.

TABLE 5-8: Applications and Awards to Women in NIST/NRC Postdoctoral Research Associateship Program, 1987-1991

Year	Total Number of Applicants	Female Applicants No.	Female Applicants %	Awards to Women (%)
1987	106	14	13.2	13.6
1988	114	14	12.3	14.3
1989	104	12	11.5	22.7
1990	121	16	13.2	16.0
1991	185	19	10.3	11.5
1992	208	25	12.0	19.4

SOURCE: Burton H. Colvin, *The NIST/NRC Postdoctoral Research Associateship Program,* paper presented at the National Research Council conference on "Science and Engineering Programs: On Target for Women?," Irvine, CA, November 4-5, 1991.

The National Institute of Standards and Technology (NIST) sponsors a Postdoctoral Research Associateship Program in chemistry, mathematics, and physics. The NIST/NRC program is not specifically an intervention or recruitment program, but its outcomes with respect to the participation of women have had the effect of interventions and are probably characteristic in many ways of the experience of the 35 other federal laboratories that participate with the NRC in similar programs (Colvin, 1991). The associateships were initiated at NIST in 1954 with positions available in three fields of mathematics, seven fields of physics, and three chemistry fields and a gross stipend of $5,940. The 1992 announcement offers 500 research opportunities with 455 different research advisers and an annual stipend of $44,000 (Colvin, 1991).

Although no special effort has been made to increase the participation of women, their percentage has, in fact, increased; for example, for the years 1987-1992, the percent of awards to women at NIST exceeded the percent of applications by women, as shown in Table 5-8. While the percentages of awards to women throughout the NRC Postdoctoral Associateship Programs are holding steady at about 20 percent, at NIST the average has been lower. The total percent of awards to women for the period

1987-1991 is 15.5 percent, compared to 9.7 percent for the period 1979-1985 (Colvin, 1991). In comparison, women received 22.8 percent of all Ph.D.s awarded in science and engineering disciplines during the 1978-1984 period and 26.2 percent in the 1985-1988 time period (NSF 1990). In the years since 1954, NIST, which has approximately 3,000 full-time employees and 1,000 guest researchers, has appointed a total of 679 research associates (about 40 percent of those in the program) to its staff. Forty-seven (7 percent) of these appointees have been women.

The CWSE conference confirmed that graduate- and postdoctoral-level interventions sponsored by the federal government are more likely to be available to women, rather than targeted to them. Nevertheless, the programs offer a wide variety of choices (Appendix A).

Future Directions

Graduate and postdoctoral interventions aimed at recruiting and retaining more women in scientific and technical fields serve the interests of sponsors and of education in general, as well as the interests of women. The model programs described above provide new ways of addressing the issues and suggest ways that elements of these programs can be replicated in other places and other situations. An important fact about them is that the models almost always include three elements identified as characteristic of successful programs: (1) specific identification of needs, (2) a total or holistic approach, with multiple linkages between graduate education and other populations, and (3) substantial faculty or mentor commitment as well as support from the head of the sponsoring organization (Fowler, 1991; Marrett, 1991; Nerad, 1991; Sheridan, 1991; Snow, 1991). This support includes commitments of both staff and money to initiate and maintain the program. An additional aspect of effective programs is opportunities for networking.

Although such programs were not part of the formal discussions at the conference on S&E programs held by the National Research Council's Committee on Women in Science and Engineering, it is important to note the existence at the graduate level of informal strategies for increasing the numbers of women receiving master's and doctorates in S&E disciplines. While often operating without commitment from, or even knowledge of, the president, the graduate dean of a university, or even (in some cases) the department head, these activities often reflect the commitment of faculty within an individual department to achieving this goal. Such interventions include active support groups where graduate students in the same or related departments meet together for discussions on how to get ahead and how to cope with daily problems in the classroom, in the research environment, and with colleagues and supervisors. They also include programs of visiting scientists and engineers, who meet with the students and other interested people to discuss and facilitate the careers of these students in science and engineering. Among recurring topics of discussion are the relationship of a female student with her peers and with her research adviser, balancing career and family responsibilities, and strategies to eliminate the "chilly environment" often encountered by women pursuing graduate studies and later employment in the sciences and engineering. During informal discussions, participants at the Conference on Science and Engineering Programs noted that the incidence of such informal programs is increasing on U.S. campuses, particularly as professional S&E societies and individual practitioners seek to encourage more women to enter S&E careers.

The replication of successful models for interventions is needed in graduate education. For example, Figure 5-5 reveals that in the sciences and engineering, only in psychology did more women receive advanced degrees than men in 1990; in general, differences between women's and men's shares of advanced degrees are particularly great at the doctoral level. Nevertheless, in spite of their potential benefits for increasing the number of women receiving graduate degrees in the sciences and engineering, efforts targeted toward women graduate students are presently extremely limited in both number and kind and are primarily in the form of recruitment and/or financial support rather than interactive retention support programs (Bogart, 1984; U.S. Congress, 1988; White House, 1989). As at the undergraduate level, "a coherent, coordinated, articulated structural approach has yet to be achieved by institutions" (Matyas and Malcolm, 1991), and little is known about the evaluation of such programs.

Listed below are some future directions for effective intervention in graduate and postdoctoral S&E education suggested by conference participants:

- "Confidence building" techniques should be developed so that women graduate students gain both scientific expertise and effective communication skills that will permit them to go forward in careers in science and mathematics with a high degree of comfort and confidence. These are clearly good skills to be developed at both the mentor/adviser and the departmental levels.

- In addition, to retain graduate students in the sciences and engineering, departments and institutions must develop programs of positive incentives for faculty. Research from numerous sources, such as the Association of American Colleges' Project on the Status and Education of Women, have shown the important role of faculty in decisions by students to continue advanced study; this is particularly true for women students in the sciences and engineering. However, unless faculty are active participants in the development of student retention programs and the faculty are rewarded for their efforts, such programs seldom achieve their goal of greater retention of women students.

- The "level playing field" concept for women graduate students must be concretely and articulately demonstrated by upper management of the academic institution. As Sandler (1986) noted, the institutional environment for women is often "chilly," particularly for women pursuing careers in "nontraditional" fields.

- At all levels—institution, department, and individual mentor— sensitivity, flexibility, and understanding of child bearing/rearing issues must be demonstrated in order to avoid discouragement and loss of talented female graduate students from these fields into others where time for a family is more easily managed. The philosophy that "it is the people, not the bricks" that make any laboratory group, department, school, or university excellent must be inculcated.

- Resolving issues related to balancing family and scientific career goals for women graduate students must be a high priority for any academic institution. This means that upper university management must do more than articulate a philosophy toward women graduate students that removes penalties or other discouragements for bearing children or even getting married. Upper management must demonstrate its commitment to putting that philosophy into action. Ideally, the institution could provide an on-site day-care facility similar to those already present at many federal laboratories and private companies and develop flexible leave policies for essential family/parenting activities. The lack of such support mechanisms is currently strong discouragement for many young graduate women scientists, mathematicians, and engineers who are attempting to balance beginning a family with graduate education.

95

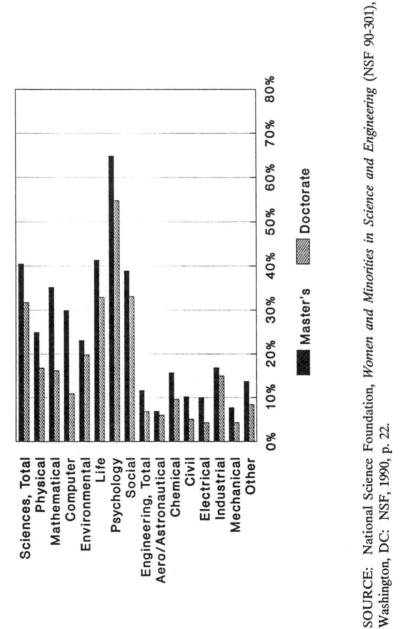

SOURCE: National Science Foundation, *Women and Minorities in Science and Engineering* (NSF 90-301), Washington, DC: NSF, 1990, p. 22.

Figure 5-5. Percentage of advanced degrees in science and engineering granted to women, by field, 1990.

Clear, flexible, and efficient policies and programs to address these concerns could benefit both female and male graduate students.

REFERENCES

Bird, Stephanie J. 1992. Personal communication to Gaelyn Davidson, July 30, 1992.

Bloch, Erich. 1988. From the director. In National Science Foundation, *Legacy to Tomorrow* (NSF 88-49), Washington, DC: U.S. Government Printing Office.

Bogart, Karen. 1984. *Toward Equity: An Action Manual for Women in Academe.* Washington, DC: Association of American Colleges.

Colvin, Burton H. 1991. *The NIST/NRC Postdoctoral Research Associateship Program.* Paper presented at the National Research Council conference on "Science and Engineering Programs: On Target for Women?" Irvine, CA, November 4-5.

Fowler, Bruce. 1991. *University of Maryland Programs in Toxicology.* Paper presented at the National Research Council conference on "Science and Engineering Programs: On Target for Women?" Irvine, CA, November 4-5.

Hall, Roberta M. 1982. *The Classroom Climate: A Chilly One for Women?* Washington, DC: Project on the Status and Education of Women, Association of American Colleges.

____, and Bernice R. Sandler. 1984. *Out of the Classroom: A Chilly Campus Climate for Women?* Washington, DC: Project on the Status and Education of Women, Association of American Colleges.

Kagiwada, Harriet H. N. 1991. *Fellowships and Societies for Women in Engineering.* Paper presented at the National Research Council conference on "Science and Engineering Programs: On Target for Women?" Irvine, CA, November 4-5.

Marrett, Cora. 1991. Discussion at the conference on "Science and Engineering Programs: On Target for Women?" Irvine, CA, November 4-5.

Matyas, Marsha Lakes, and Malcom, Shirley M. (eds.). 1991. *Investing in Human Potential: Science and Engineering at the Crossroads.* Washington, DC: American Association for the Advancement of Science.

National Science Board. 1991. *Science & Engineering Indicators: 1991* (Tenth Edition) (NSF 91-1), Washington, DC: NSF.

National Science Foundation (NSF). 1988. *Legacy to Tomorrow* (NSF 88-49), Washington, DC: U.S. Government Printing Office.

_____. 1990. *Women and Minorities in Science and Engineering* (NSF 90-301). Washington, DC: NSF.

_____. 1992. *America's Academic Future: A Report of the Presidential Young Investigator Colloquium on U.S. Engineering, Mathematics, and Science Education for the Year 2010 and Beyond* (NSF 91-150). Washington, DC: NSF.

Nerad, Maresi. 1991. *Using Time, Money, and Human Resources Efficiently and Effectively in the Case of Women Graduate Students.* Conference on "Science and Engineering Programs: On Target for Women?" Irvine, CA, November 4-5.

_____, and Joseph Cerny. 1991. From facts to action: Expanding the educational role of the graduate division. *CGS Communicator* **May**:8. Washington, DC: Council of Graduate Schools in the United States.

Ruppenthal, Karol. 1991. Summary presentation, session on graduate education at the conference on "Science and Engineering Programs: On Target for Women?" Irvine, CA, November 4-5.

Sandler, Bernice R. 1986. *The Campus Climate Revisited: Chilly for Women Faculty, Administrators, and Graduate Students.* Washington, DC: Project on the Status and Education of Women, Association of American Colleges.

Sheridan, Judson D. 1991. *Intervention Programs at the University of Missouri-Columbia.* Paper presented at the National Research Council conference on "Science and Engineering Programs: On Target for Women?" Irvine, CA, November 4-5.

Sloan Foundation. 1991. *Project Summaries.* Conference on Science and Engineering Education, New York, July 23.

Snow, L. Nan. 1991. *The National Physical Science Consortium.* Paper presented at the National Research Council conference on "Science and Engineering Programs: On Target for Women?" Irvine, CA, November 4-5.

U.S. Congress, Office of Technology Assessment. 1988. *Educating Scientists and Engineers: Grade School to Grad School* (OTA-SET-377). Washington, DC: U.S. Government Printing Office.

White House Task Force on Women, Minorities, and the Handicapped in Science and Technology. 1989. *Changing America: The New Face of Science and Technology* (Final Report). Washington, DC: The Task Force.

EMPLOYMENT

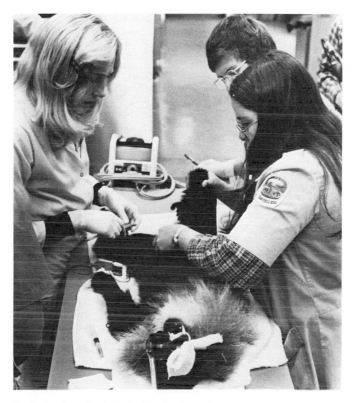

Reproductive physiologist Dr. Barbara Durrant, curator of primates Diane Brockman, and veterinarian Dr. Jane Meier prepare a lion-tailed macaque for artificial insemination at the San Diego Zoo Hospital.
(Photo: Zoological Society of San Diego)

6

PROMOTING SCIENCE AND ENGINEERING CAREERS IN ACADEME

Garrison Sposito

Garrison Sposito is Professor of Soil Physical Chemistry in the University of California at Berkeley. A graduate of the University of Arizona, he earned a Ph.D. in Soil Science at Berkeley and taught in both the California State University system and the University of California system before assuming his present position in 1988. He has been active in research and teaching in soil and water sciences and most recently was involved with national committees charged with setting future basic research agendas for these two disciplines of earth science.

Professor Sposito has been involved in gender-related issues through participation on the Executive Committee of the Center for the Teaching and Study of American Cultures at Berkeley. On a more personal level, he has maintained an equal participation of women and men in his research group (graduate students, postdoctoral researchers, etc.) since 1980, when he first became fully aware of some of the issues discussed in this chapter.

Women on Science and Engineering Faculties

Public awareness continues to grow concerning the many contributions of women to science and engineering research, particularly those women who serve on the faculties of universities (Hoffman, 1991). Despite improving media coverage and a continual increase in the number of women who elect to pursue doctoral (or medical) degrees in science and engineering fields (CWSE, 1991; Hays, 1991), a disappointing, static picture emerges of the career patterns of women in academe. For example, about two-thirds of the women now on science or engineering faculties do not have tenure, whereas something less than 40 percent of the male faculty members now are untenured (Figure 6-1). This discrepancy is much greater in the major research universities, where both the percentage and the absolute number of women who hold the rank of professor or associate professor are very low

101

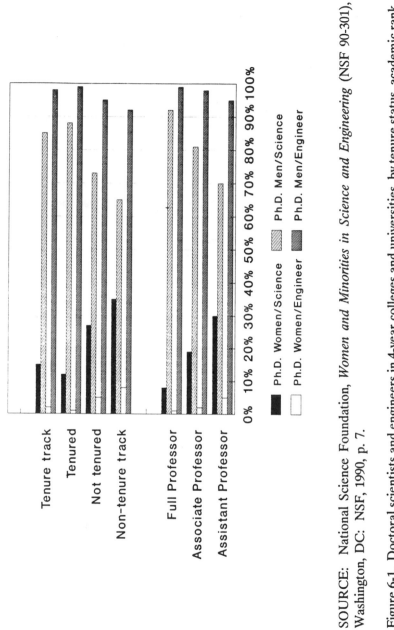

SOURCE: National Science Foundation, *Women and Minorities in Science and Engineering* (NSF 90-301), Washington, DC: NSF, 1990, p. 7.

Figure 6-1. Doctoral scientists and engineers in 4-year colleges and universities, by tenure status, academic rank, and sex, 1987.

indeed (CWSE, 1991). Thus, although the "pipeline" into academe for women shows general increases in size and improvements in visibility, these trends have been slower and lower than would have been expected from the Ph.D. pool (CWSE, 1991; Brush, 1991).

What Are the Generic Issues?

Career-related statistics for women in academe can vary greatly across scientific and engineering fields. [For example, in the University of California system, 105 of the 1,000 tenured faculty members in the life sciences are women, but there are only 47 women among the 1,000 tenured physical sciences/mathematics professors (Cota-Robles, 1991).] Some of this variability is related directly to issues that are of a particular nature: the public image of a specific field; its visibility to science and engineering majors as a career opportunity; the demand for it in the private sector; and its distribution among the academic programs of doctorate-granting universities. These issues are perhaps of lesser importance than the broad, generic issues that affect most, if not all, career patterns of women scientists and engineers who choose to work in higher education. It is the generic issues that interventions are expected to address first and foremost (CWSE, 1991). And, as can be seen in Figure 6-2, interventions are necessary to increase the low percentage of S&E faculty who are women.

The "Glass Ceiling"

Many data are available to show that the rate of advancement of women in academe is significantly less than that of men, even when the comparison is normalized for educational background, years of professional experience, or research productivity (CWSE, 1991; Brush, 1991). This now incontestable fact indicates that an implicit barrier to advancement a "glass ceiling"—exists for women faculty members. Given the persistent, low percentages of women who become tenured on science and engineering faculties, despite enlargement of the pool of female applicants for entry-level appointments, the tentative conclusion can be drawn that the "glass ceiling" operates at the associate professor rank in most research universities.

The "Rules of the Game"

Brush (1991) alludes to a network of expectations, conceptual dogmas, and social interactions that may underlie the functioning of academic departments on a daily basis and to which allegiance is required in order that

103

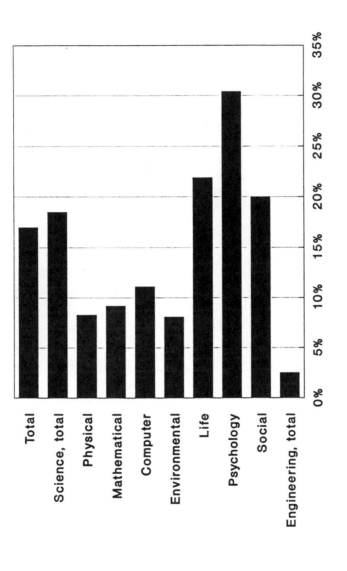

SOURCE: National Science Foundation, *Women and Minorities in Science and Engineering* (NSF 90-301), Washington, DC: NSF, 1990, Appendix B, Tables 16 and 18.

Figure 6-2. Percentage of women science and engineering faculty at U.S. institutions, 1987.

a faculty member achieve success. These unwritten "rules of the game" must become known to the aspiring assistant professor very soon after appointment to ensure a smooth passage to tenure. Aisenberg and Harrington (1988) have described poignantly how often the "rules of the game" go unlearned by women in academe until professional disaster strikes. They cite a series of homely counsels, distilled from many telling experiences, that can help to alleviate this problem: assume there will be opposition; be persistent; learn to say "no"; use contacts; choose your fights. Perhaps most revealing of the anecdotal information given to them about how to travel safely along the road to tenure was that provided by a woman newly-promoted to associate professor. "I was very lucky," she related, "to have a female chairperson who took me through tenure the way you would want a mother to stand by you as a guide, who really cared about you but wanted you to have your own independence" (Aisenberg and Harrington, 1988, p. 47).

The "Biological Clock"

Most of the recent literature on career patterns of women scientists and engineers reviews the perennial issue of the apparent conflict between the demands of motherhood (or other familial obligations) and those of the profession (Aisenberg and Harrington, 1988; Brush, 1991). This conflict has taken an especially acute form in the context of academe because of the requirements for tenure (CWSE, 1991). Although fast disappearing into retirement are the senior male professors who expound the antediluvian views that women faculty members with children dilute academic research productivity, or that women faculty members should not bear children, most universities do not function in practice as if these views were passé. Recognition of the "biological clock" and, more generally, of a faculty member's familial obligations is still treated as a variance to normal professional activity instead of as an integral part of it.

These three generic issues do not exhaust the tableau of problems that face women who choose careers in academe to do teaching and research in scientific or engineering fields. But they do surface repeatedly in a number of recent self-evaluations undertaken by major research universities to assess the academic environment for women on science faculties. The principal findings in these studies echo the concerns noted above:

- With few exceptions women in science are but a small minority in their peer groups, and their

105

proportion drops sharply as they advance through their careers. The resulting isolation impedes research, increases stress, and may lead to abandonment of a scientific career.

- The period when successful scientific careers are usually forged (in the general career pattern developed when the enterprise was almost exclusively male) corresponds to the period of childbearing.
- Experimental work, which makes extraordinary demands on availability in time or location, raises conflicts with the family responsibilities that continue to be disproportionately borne by women.
- Women graduate students are often dissuaded from pursuing certain areas of science. In some disciplines they are discouraged by faculty and student colleagues from pursuing mathematical or theoretical investigations; in other fields women are discouraged from pursuing experimental work (Wilson, 1992).

Recognition of these issues and their importance to the success or failure of women scientists in academe as part of the basis for designing interventions was one of the discussion themes at the Irvine conference. Such recognition can serve as a reference frame from which to evaluate the options and effectiveness of the model interventions that were presented at the Irvine conference and are summarized in the following sections.

Sample Interventions

Table 6-1 recapitulates key features of five interventions about which information was provided at the Irvine conference. Perusal of the table indicates that all the programs address enhancing the research capability and competitiveness of their targeted groups. Most of the programs are directed toward scientists and engineers who are in an early stage of their careers. Almost none of the programs are directed uniquely at women faculty members and some—indeed, half of those listed in the table—have no emphasis on women at all. In this respect, the programs of the National Science Foundation (NSF) perhaps deserve a more detailed exposition, since they contain at least a specific reference to women faculty.

Programs at NSF

Visiting Professorships for Women (VPW). This program provides opportunities for postdoctoral women engineers and scientists who (1) work in the disciplines supported by NSF, (2) are employed in industry, government, professional associations, and academic institutions, or (3) are established, published, independent scholars to advance their careers via independent research and to serve as role models and provide motivation, guidance, and encouragement for women students to pursue careers in science and engineering. The VPW program enables women scientists and engineers to undertake research and other activities, including teaching, at host academic institutions in the United States, its possessions, or territories. These may be either universities or four-year colleges where the necessary facilities and resources can be made available. The visiting professor's activities should:

- contribute to the body of scientific knowledge through her research,
- enhance the research and instructional programs of the host institution,
- affect women students at the host institution who may be planning careers in science and engineering, and
- benefit the home institution by increasing the skills of the returning staff member.

The research may be conducted independently or in collaboration with others, but more than half of the award period should be spent on the research activities.

The visiting professor is expected to serve as a role model and provide explicit guidance and encouragement to other women seeking to pursue careers in science or engineering. She undertakes teaching, counseling and mentoring, and/or other interactive outreach activities to increase the visibility of women scientists and engineers in the academic environment of the host institution, and to demonstrate to students opportunities for careers in science and engineering. These interactive activities may be at the undergraduate or graduate level, be directed to the community at large, or involve some combination of such activities.

107

TABLE 6-1: Summary Features of Some Targeted Intervention Programs

Program and Supporting Agency

♦ *National Science Foundation* (Klein, 1991)
Visiting Professorships (VPW)

Faculty Awards (FAW)

Career Advancement Awards (CAA)

Research Planning Grants (RPG)

♦ *University of California* (Cota-Robles and González, 1991)
President's Postdoctoral Fellowships

Academic Career Development Program for Minorities
and Women

♦ *National Institute of General Medical Sciences* (Maddox, 1991)
Minority Biomedical Research Support (MBRS)

Minority Access to Research Careers (MARC)

♦ *National Aeronautics and Space Administration* (McGee, 1991)
Resident Research Associateships

Summer Faculty Fellowships

♦ *Department of Veterans Affairs* (Hays, 1991)
Research Career Development

Designed To Enhance Career Opportunities in Science and Engineering

Targeted Groups	Relevance to Women in Academe
Women scientists and engineers	Enhance research skills and role modeling
Tenured women faculty in science and engineering	Research support for "outstanding women faculty"
Experienced women faculty scientists and engineers	Enhance research career potential
Women scientists and engineers	Facilitate competitive research proposals
Women and racial or ethnic minorities	Enhance competitiveness for faculty appointment in universities and colleges
Women and racial or ethnic minorities	Prepare for academic careers
Faculty at institutions with substantial minority enrollments	No special emphasis
Students and faculty at institutions with substantial minority onrollments	No special emphasis
Postdoctoral scientists and engineers	No direct relevance
Recently-appointed faculty at teaching institutions	No direct relevance
Medical clinicians and investigators	No direct relevance

Faculty Awards for Women (FAW). This program recognizes "outstanding women faculty" nominated by their academic institutions through the provision of research awards. Nominees must be tenured but not hold the rank of professor. In FY 1991, 601 nominations were received and 100 awards were made. The number of nominations represents about 8% of the female associate professors in science and engineering in the United States. About 80% of the awards were roughly equally divided among the physical sciences, biological sciences, and engineering, with the remaining 20% shared by geological and computer sciences.

Career Advancement Awards (CAA). This program—open to experienced, postdoctoral investigators who are scientists and engineers—is designed to expand research opportunities for women by helping researchers acquire expertise in new areas to enhance their research capability and by assisting those who have had a significant research career interruption to acquire "updating" for re-entry into their respective fields. Awards may be used for salary (summer and release time, if it can be justified), professional travel, consultant fees, research assistants, and other research-related expenses, including equipment. Eligibility is limited to women scientists and engineers in an NSF-supported field who hold faculty (not necessarily tenure-track) or research-related positions in U.S. colleges, universities, or related institutions and have had some prior independent research experience as principal investigators or project leaders.

Research Planning Grants (RPG). This program, on the other hand, is designed to increase the number of new women investigators participating in NSF research programs and to facilitate preliminary studies and other activities related to the development of competitive research projects and proposals by women who have not previously had independent federal research funding. These are one-time awards that may be used for preliminary work to determine the feasibility of a proposed line of inquiry and/or for other activities that will facilitate proposal development. These awards may include summer salary; released time; professional travel; consultant fees; and other research-related expenses that would enhance the quality of the proposed research.

Other Interventions

President's Postdoctoral Fellowship Program. This program, initiated in 1984 by the Office of the President of the University of California, was

110

designed to increase the competitiveness of women and racial or ethnic minority Ph.D. degree recipients for faculty appointments at the University of California and other major institutions of higher education (Cota-Robles and González, 1991). The program currently offers up to two years of support for postdoctoral research for each of 20 new Fellows per year. Each Fellow has a faculty sponsor who provides mentoring and guidance and who helps promote the Fellow's visibility among colleagues on other campuses.

Since the program began, 1,455 persons have applied for President's Fellowships. Of these applicants, 138 have received fellowships, 76 of them women. As of 1991, 98 Fellows had completed the two-year program; 52 of them, of whom 31 are women, had obtained tenure-track appointments at universities.

Academic Career Development Program (ACDP). Another program instituted throughout the University of California system to prepare women and minorities for careers in academe is the ACDP, "an integrated program of support" having four components: (1) Graduate Outreach and Recruitment, (2) Graduate Mentorship Awards, (3) Research Assistantships/Mentorships, and (4) Dissertation-Year Fellowships (University of California, 1991). Each component focuses on a particular activity to enhance graduate retention and promote academic careers:

- Graduate Outreach and Recruitment: Potential students visit and participate in summer internship programs in university departments. In 1990, 226 undergraduates from the University of California (UC), 43 from California State University, and 137 from other institutions participated in the summer programs at all nine UC campuses.
- Graduate Mentorship Awards: Outstanding minority and women Ph.D. students work with faculty mentors in selecting courses of study and developing dissertation topics. In academic year 1990-91, all 67 students who had received awards in 1989-90 continued the program, along with 68 starting the first of two years.
- Graduate Research Assistantship/Mentorship Program: Minority and women graduate students work half-time as research assistants, reducing their reliance on loans and providing opportunities for them to engage in intensive research. In academic year 1989-90, 100 women and minority graduate students participated in this program; 104 were enrolled in 1990-91.
- Dissertation-Year Fellowship Program: An annual stipend of $12,000

111

plus $500 for research expenses enables women and minorities who are Ph.D. candidates to complete their theses and prepare for faculty teaching positions. Since 1986, 177 students (68 men and 109 women) have received these fellowships. Of the 84 fellows who have earned their Ph.D.s, 38 have received tenure-track positions, and 21 are pursuing postdoctoral research.

Although the program is relatively new, initial evaluations of each component have indicated their success in helping the University of California to attract outstanding students from throughout the country (University of California, 1991).

Minority Biomedical Research Support (MBRS). This program of the National Institute of General Medical Sciences focuses on increasing the number of minority biomedical research scientists and on the recruitment of underrepresented minorities into undergraduate and graduate science programs (Maddox, 1991). Experience with these programs suggests that recruitment efforts designed to encourage and increase underrepresented populations into the sciences are not only similar, but, perhaps, universal. Thus, it may be possible to utilize the same approach to enhance specifically the number of women in the sciences. Prior to the availability of MBRS grants, members of minority science faculties in the Historically Black Colleges and Universities (HBCUs) were not encouraged to apply for federal research funds. Many had received doctoral training in majority institutions under professors who had federally funded grants but, when these minority scientists assumed faculty positions at an HBCU, a variety of factors operated against continuation of their research interests through independently sponsored projects. A combination of long teaching hours, lack of modern facilities and equipment, lack of information about funding sources, lack of grantsmanship and guidance in seeking funding, and, most of all, frustration, disillusionment and lack of faith in the "the system" took their toll. Similar frustrations are experienced by women wishing to pursue careers in academe (Aisenberg and Harrington, 1988). It was through the efforts of several advocates for strengthening minority representation in education that the idea for the development of biomedical research support for predominately black colleges was conceptualized. The predominant funding instrument, the traditional MBRS grant, is awarded to faculty members at qualifying institutions (two- and four-year colleges) for biomedical research projects that employ students, both undergraduate and graduate, as part of the supported

112

research team. A special feature of the traditional MBRS grant is the participation of Associate Investigator Institutions. These are majority institutions that grant the Ph.D. degree and have established investigators with National Institutes of Health (NIH) support who are eager to work either with students at an HBCU or with minority students at their own institution. These investigators participate in the MBRS grant, but receive funds only for student-related costs. In addition, the program offers support for certain types of renovation projects and the purchase of research equipment.

Evaluations of the MBRS program has shown its effectiveness in recruiting minority students to careers in scientific research (see, for example, Garrison and Brown, 1985).

On Target for Women?

The interventions summarized in Table 6-1 vary widely in their relevance to women faculty in science and engineering. On the one hand, NASA sponsors only pre-baccalaureate programs targeted to women, and its faculty research programs, like those of the Department of Veterans Affairs, not only do not place any special emphasis on women, but may even be structured so rigidly vis-à-vis work hours and child care issues that they actually inhibit participation by female professors (McGee, 1991; Hays, 1991). On the other hand, the NSF programs, although structured and administered like any other of its research opportunity programs, are targeted directly to women scientists and engineers, in some cases to junior faculty members whose research experience is limited (CAA and RPG programs). Still other programs (President's Fellowships and MBRS programs) offer advantages to women contemplating academic careers while not targeting them specifically. It appears that none of the programs summarized in Table 6-1 were *designed by women faculty members for women faculty members*, existing or prospective (Sposito, 1991). In this respect, it can be said that, effectively, no programs of major proportions are available solely to promote the careers of women scientists and engineers in academe.

To what degree is this statement an unfair judgment? It is not unfair as a conclusion in respect to the highly competitive, time-demanding, federal research enhancement programs whose structuring simply ignores the multifaceted lifestyle of women professors (Aisenberg and Harrington, 1988) in favor of a one-dimensional ideal of the scientist-academic as workaholic and polemist extraordinaire (Brush, 1991). Indeed, as Linda Wilson (1992)

113

pointed out in her recent testimony before the House Subcommittee on Employment Opportunities,

> More subtle forms of discrimination also continue, including, for example, treatment of women as outsiders and negative attitudes of faculty toward women's family commitments. The male dominance of the tenured science faculty in major research universities results in many non-tenured women feeling powerless. Many non-tenured women do not have positive, collegial relationships with senior members of their departments and are deprived of the mentoring relationships that are often critical to advancement in a field. In some cases, junior faculty feel exploited; and in many cases, women perceive their situations to be worse than those of their male junior colleagues. The failure to integrate junior faculty within their own department has been a long-standing problem in some cases.
> Many institutions have recently undertaken studies of access and the environment for women. These efforts are commendable, but the studies frequently show that the same barriers and problems found in similar reviews 20 years ago still persist.
> Most of these problems reflect a culture that has insufficiently recognized the capabilities and contributions of women and their potential, a culture that has not kept pace with women's changing employment patterns and society's increasing need for women scientists' talent. These problems are a result of our tendency to imagine the ideal scientist as a man who can single-mindedly devote 80 hours a week to science because he has no conflicting familial obligations.

It is unfair, however, to overlook the essential, positive features of some programs that, although not addressing directly the three generic issues raised above, do contain ingredients with which a successful approach to promoting the careers of women faculty members can be fashioned:

- *mentoring*, said repeatedly in the Irvine conference to be critical (and

114

always successful experientially, if not strictly in professional terms) to achieving the self-confidence necessary for realizing the goals of any enhancement program;

- *networking*, communicating frequently with peers in order to "find out what's going on," gain political skills, and obtain continual reassurance that the difficulties one faces are not unique or insurmountable; and
- *strongly supportive top management*, without which programs to enhance the careers of women faculty are doomed to be short-term, under-financed, and subject to inconsistent resource allocations that actually signal low institutional commitment. It is well to remember that statements from an administration about resource availability are actually statements about the relative priorities of the administration.

Women are not being appointed at expected rates or promoted to expected levels. Among the reasons given for the slow and low rates of women's advancement up the academic career ladder in science and engineering are the following: geographic constraints on dual-career families, narrowness of searches to fill faculty openings, fears that the department will not be getting its due because of family commitments, and lack of "top-down" support within the institution.

Future Directions

Given the disappointing paucity of major interventions to promote the careers of women scientists and engineers in academe, the Irvine conference discussion focused on strategies to develop these programs at the university level. Following are four broad strategies whose implementation by universities would do much to address the three generic issues described above.

1 **Establish an Office on the Status of Women Faculty Members, whose director is a senior female professor with line responsibility to the chief administrative officer of the campus.**

The responsibilities of the director should include:

- data-taking and monitoring regarding all appointments, merit advancements, and grievance claims of women faculty members;

115

- facilitating networking among women faculty members on the campus; and
- designing (with the help of tenured women faculty members) and implementing mentored interventions for untenured women faculty members.

2   **Revise the tenure process on campus.**

The faculty governing body (academic senate) on campus should revise the tenure process to ensure that untenured women faculty members are indeed reviewed by their peers during the probationary period. "Peer review" does not simply constitute an evaluation of the prima facie productivity and quality of research or teaching. It means an evaluation based on a deep, palpable understanding of what it means experientially to be a woman on the faculty. This kind of understanding among male faculty members has long been a facet of their tenure review processes. The same tacit, mutual sharing of academic and social values must now be ensured to occur for women faculty members, and this cannot happen until *every tenure-review committee has at least one female member.* Brush (1991) has described other reforms of the probationary process that will ensure that women are treated equitably, most of them having to do with their family responsibilities. The University of California (1991) recently has begun to explore a much broader definition of the criteria for merit advancement that goes a long way toward reforming the tenure process in research universities. It specifically recognizes mentoring of students or junior faculty by professors as an integral part of the teaching responsibility and the reward structure.

3   **Create a family-friendly workplace environment.**

The chief administrative officer of the campus must recognize officially the fundamental role that family plays in the lives of women and men faculty members by taking steps to ensure as full an integration as possible of family and professional responsibilities in the workplace environment. Professors who are women (or men, for that matter) must no longer have to endure extraordinary stress in their daily lives by attempting to meet these responsibilities in a work environment that wishes to pretend that only narrowly-defined professional activities are important (Aisenberg and Harrington, 1988). As one Irvine conference attendee put it, "The time is over when faculty members who are new mothers should have to hide the breast

116

pump under their desks." Steps must be taken to establish flexible work schedules, job sharing, and fully subsidized, proximate child care as *standard* features of campus programs for the faculty.

4   Allow maximum flexibility in working conditions, consistent with carrying out responsibilities of teaching and research.

As pointed out during the discussions of both academic and industrial employment at the CWSE Conference on Science and Engineering Programs, greater flexibility may require additional expense but should be cost-effective in terms of the productivity of S&E employees. Universities could be expected to profit by implementation of some practices, such as offering flexible benefits packages, becoming more common in industry.

REFERENCES

Aisenberg, N., and M. Harrington. 1988. *Women of Academe: Outsiders in the Sacred Grove.* Amherst: University of Massachusetts Press.

Brush, Stephen G. 1991. Women in science and engineering. *American Scientist* 79:404-419.

Committee on Women in Science and Engineering (CWSE). 1991. *Women in Science and Engineering: Increasing Their Numbers in the 1990s.* Washington, DC: National Academy Press.

Cota-Robles, Eugene H. 1991. Personal communication, November 4, 1991.

_____, and J. González. 1991. *The President's Postdoctoral Fellowship Program.* Paper presented at the National Research Council conference on "Science and Engineering Programs: On Target for Women?" Irvine, CA, November 4-5.

Garrison, Howard H., and Prudence W. Brown. 1985. *Minority Access to Research Careers: An Evaluation of the Honors Undergraduate Research Training Program.* Washington, DC: National Academy Press.

Hays, Marguerite T. 1991. *The VA's Research Career Development Program as an Opportunity for Women to Enter Medical Research.* Paper presented at the National Research Council conference on "Science and Engineering Programs: On Target for Women?" Irvine, CA, November 4-5.

Hoffman, Paul (ed.). 1991. *Discover* **12**(10). Special Issue: A Celebration of Women in Science. New York: The Walt Disney Company.

Klein, Margrete S. 1991. *NSF Programs for Women*. Paper prepared for the National Research Council conference on "Science and Engineering Programs: On Target for Women?" Irvine, CA, November 4-5.

Maddox, Yvonne T. 1991. *Promoting Careers in Academe: National Institute of General Medical Sciences Minority Programs*. Paper presented at the National Research Council conference on "Science and Engineering Programs: On Target for Women?" Irvine, CA, November 4-5.

McGee, Sherri. 1991. *Promoting Careers in Academe: Opportunities at NASA for College and University Faculty*. Paper presented at the National Research Council conference on "Science and Engineering Programs: On Target for Women?" Irvine, CA, November 4-5.

Sposito, Garrison. 1991. Personal communication with participants at the conference, "Science and Engineering Programs: On Target for Women?" Irvine, CA, November 4-5.

University of California (UC), Office of the President. 1991. *Report on Affirmative Action Programs for University Academic Employees and Graduate and Professional Students*. UC: Oakland.

Wilson, Linda S. 1992. Testimony during the Oversight Hearing on Sexual Harassment in Non-Traditional Occupations, United States House of Representatives, Committee on Education and Labor, Subcommittee on Employment Opportunities, Washington, DC, June 25.

7

PROMOTING SCIENCE AND ENGINEERING CAREERS IN INDUSTRY

Esther M. Conwell

Esther Conwell is a Research Fellow at the Xerox Research Laboratories in Webster, NY, where she currently works on electronic properties of conducting polymers and other topics in condensed matter physics. She is also an adjunct professor in the Chemistry Department at the University of Rochester and an Associate Director of the NSF Science and Technology Center for Photoinduced Charge Transfer located at the University.

After earning a Ph.D. in physics from the University of Chicago, she taught for some years at Brooklyn College. Most of her career since then has been in industrial laboratories, first GTE Labs and then Xerox. Dr. Conwell has a large number of publications in various fields of condensed matter physics and is a member of the National Academy of Sciences and the National Academy of Engineering. After a number of years on the advisory board of the Office of Scientific and Engineering Personnel (OSEP), she was appointed to the National Research Council's Committee on Women in Science and Engineering.

Background

Women comprise approximately 16 percent of the scientists and engineers employed in industry, 28 percent of the scientists and 4 percent of the engineers (Figure 7-1). At present, more women hold bachelor's degrees than advanced degrees in science and engineering. While both men and women scientists and engineers are more likely to be found in the life sciences, their distribution across other disciplines varies significantly, with women being concentrated in psychology and the social sciences and men more often found in engineering and the physical sciences (Figure 7-2). Women scientists and engineers are more likely to be unemployed (Figure 7-3) and underutilized than their male counterparts. Once employed, women in industry face both lower salaries than their male peers (Figure 7-4) and invisible barriers—the "glass ceiling" and the "glass wall"—to vertical and

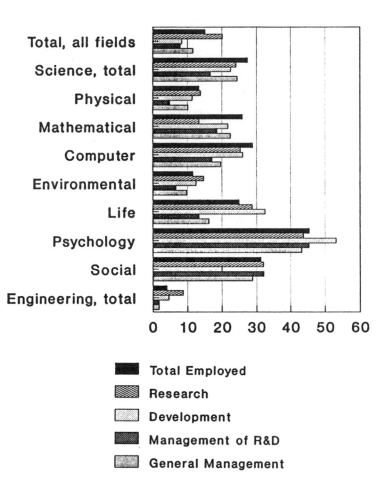

Total, all fields
Science, total
Physical
Mathematical
Computer
Environmental
Life
Psychology
Social
Engineering, total

0   10   20   30   40   50   60

- ■ Total Employed
- ▨ Research
- □ Development
- ▩ Management of R&D
- ▨ General Management

SOURCE: National Science Foundation, *Women and Minorities in Science and Engineering* (NSF 90-301), Washington, DC: NSF, 1990, Appendix B, Tables 13 and 15.

Figure 7-1. Percentage of industrially employed women scientists and engineers, at all degree levels, by field and selected primary work activity, 1986.

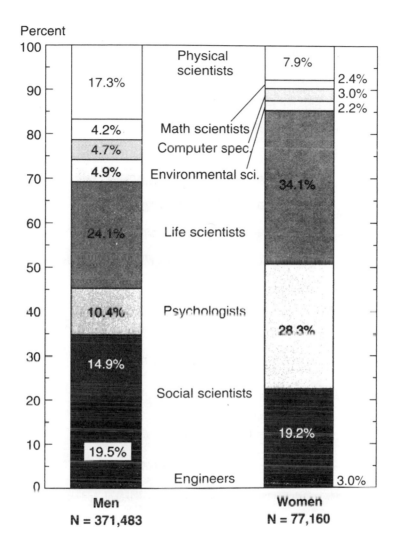

SOURCE: National Science Board, *Science & Engineering Indicators—1991* (NSB 91-1), Washington, DC: U.S. Government Printing Office, 1991.

Figure 7-2. Distribution of employed doctoral scientists and engineers, by field and sex, 1989.

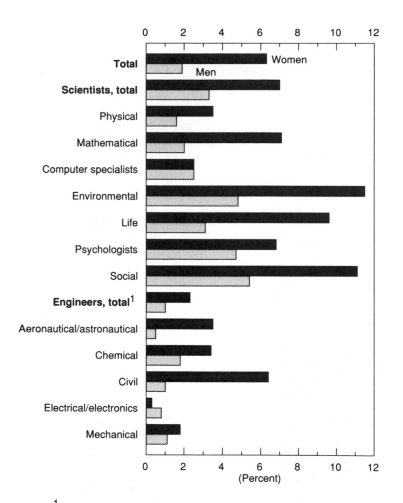

SOURCE: National Science Foundation, *Women and Minorities in Science and Engineering* (NSF 90-301), Washington, DC: NSF, 1990.

Figure 7-3. Science and engineering unemployment rates of men and women, by field, 1986.

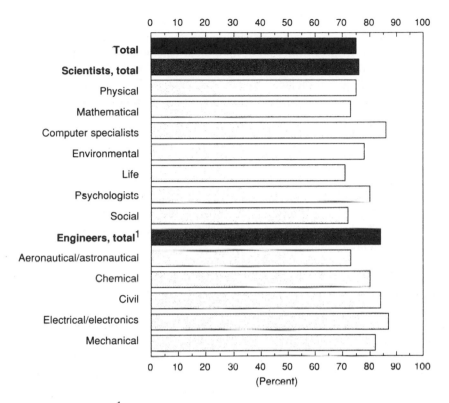

¹Includes industrial, materials, mining, nuclear, petroleum, and other.

SOURCE: National Science Foundation, *Women and Minorities in Science and Engineering* (NSF 90-301), Washington, DC: NSF, 1990.

Figure 7-4. Women's salaries as a percentage of men's salaries, by field, 1986.

lateral movement in the corporate structure. A recent study by the U.S. Department of Labor (1991) noted:

> In general, many corporations identify key employees—often early in their careers—and oversee their career advancement through yearly appraisals and needs

123

assessments. Such assessment systems may include identification of such individuals as "high potentials" and include forms of internal development (including rotational assignments, mentoring and training), external development (including graduate studies, executive development programs), international assignments, and highly visible positions (such as special assistants to senior executives, and assignments to corporate task forces and committees). These serve as available means to give key contributors experiences to enhance their academic and work-related credentials.

While these practices generally benefit the corporate employee, they can serve to impede the advancement of qualified minorities and women if they are not inclusive of all human talent.

The challenges of increasing competition and declining numbers in the traditional white male pool, however, are beginning to force corporations to recruit, retain, and develop the talents of women at every level. This is true for positions in science and engineering as well as management positions. Some companies have developed good programs for recruiting and retaining women scientists and engineers. Since less is known about this type of intervention than programs in academe, for example, we begin this chapter with a description of a few of these programs. Successful corporate models appear to have certain characteristics in common:

- high-level support, up to and including the CEO level,
- mentoring programs that are institutionalized and continuing,
- grass roots efforts, such as internal women's self-help or networking groups,
- an open corporate culture that permits such job options as flex time, part-time, job sharing, and work at home,
- institutionalized efforts to create gender sensitivity in the workplace, such as training programs on "diversity" and gender-related issues, and incentives and accountability for managers on these issues, and
- continuing program evaluations in terms of keeping data on recruitment and retention rates and attitudes of women toward their work.

124

Sample Programs[1]

The 1991 CWSE-sponsored conference on S&E interventions showcased programs in three large manufacturing companies—Hughes Aircraft Company (a subsidiary of General Motors), Corning, and Xerox—to illustrate what, by current standards, are programs well designed to recruit and ensure the professional progress of women in the companies. In the cases of Corning and Xerox, a sizable part of the programs described focused on corporate research and development (R&D).

Underlying the programs for women in these three companies is an assumption at the top levels of management that (1) the upcoming changes in the composition of the work force mean that, to be competitive in the future, technical companies will need more women scientists and engineers and (2) to get maximum productivity they must remove obstacles that limit women's performance. Thus, the major justification presented for special programs to recruit and retain women scientists and engineers in these companies is the bottom line, the future profitability of the company. In line with this, the corporate slogans have changed from "affirmative action" to "work force diversity."

Hughes Aircraft Company

This company believes women "to be one of the most successful resources to address some of the projected shortfalls in engineering and scientific personnel" (Frownfelter, 1991). Nevertheless, retention of women employees is an important problem for Hughes, even though the company has been actively recruiting, encouraging career advancement, and promoting women in scientific and engineering disciplines for more than 30 years

---

[1]Careers of women scientists and engineers in industry is, of course, a broad subject, which will be the focus of the January 17-18, 1993, conference of the Committee on Women in Science and Engineering. The Committee recognizes that intervention strategies employed by the larger U.S. firms may be inappropriate in smaller companies and will strive to present a balance of programs—based on company size, product, and mission—at the 1993 conference. In addition, both manufacturing- and service-oriented companies will be represented at that conference.

125

(Frownfelter, 1991). The company has recently improved recruitment rates by using three basic approaches to the problem:

1   increasing external visibility of career opportunities within the company for women engineers and scientists,
2   increasing interaction with other companies and other industries, and
3   increasing the company's visibility in the community and proactive women's organizations.

In general, the company has found it more effective to aim its efforts at work groups and their interrelationships rather than at individuals (Frownfelter, 1991).

Currently, there are 3,100 women in scientific and engineering endeavors at Hughes, representing 15 percent of the technical work force. The total Hughes work force, not including subsidiaries, is about 49,000, of which 17,000 are women. Some 10 percent of the technical management and about 5 percent of the executive management are women. According to Frownfelter (1991), in 1992 the company will probably hire between 2000 and 3000 professionals (while simultaneously downsizing by a comparable number to accomplish a shift of emphasis from defense to commercial electronics work). The company's goal is to have women comprise 50 percent of new hires. Hughes measures the success of its programs "by periodically monitoring the number of its women employees."

Among measures Hughes has taken to attract and retain women is development of role models and mentoring. The company considers role models of great importance for motivating women and showing them what their possibilities can be. If there are no visible role models, management creates them by promoting from within or bringing in women at a high level from outside. Support groups committed to counseling and team problem solving also play a mentoring role. Training of managers is also given high importance. All managers are required to take 16 hours of training a year in work force diversity management, including mentoring training.

There are three active, formal technical women's groups at Hughes. The groups were started by individual women employees whose grassroots efforts received official company recognition after the groups had been in existence for about two years. One of the groups, the Intergroup Women's Forum, is a cross-organizational group developed to provide both technological and personal communication and visibility throughout the company. A second group with similar aims includes women in spacecraft and communications technology. The third group is affiliated with the Society of Women Engineers. The groups are very much involved in the development of career counseling and act as a mentoring network. The groups are allocated work time to meet once a month, but meet more often on their own time. Agendas include technical work problems, but also child care and carpooling arrangements.

Even though women are still underrepresented in the Hughes work force, the company believes it has established a good base on which to build.

Corning Corporation

Corning has a long-standing commitment to achieving diversity in its work force, including specific targets for improvement in numbers of women in its exempt ranks (Menger, 1991). As do many companies, Corning carries out "climate surveys" of employee attitudes every two years, and managers receive the results in averaged formats to retain confidentiality. In 1987 the company survey indicated considerably lower job satisfaction among women than men, particularly for women in the Research, Development, and Engineering (RD&E) division of the company. At the same time, the attrition rate for women in the corporation was 15 percent, or three times that for men, a rate representing considerable expense to the company (Figure 7-5). In an effort to address these problems, the company formed a Corrective Action Team (CAT), made up of both men and women. The group met weekly and ultimately recommended a number of actions intended to improve the working climate for women. Among the programs that were established as a result of the CAT recommendations are:

- the Corning Professional Women's Forum, which meets regularly and provides an important network for women employees (the Forum also brings in speakers and publishes a newsletter containing information of particular interest to women employees),
- targets for increasing the number of women in higher level jobs,
- Parent Resource and Referral Center to provide quality child-care services for all employees and others in the community (the service was established jointly with the school board and other community organizations),

127

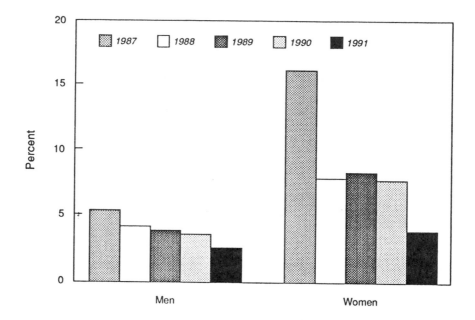

SOURCE: Eve L. Menger, *Selected Employee Retention Efforts at Corning Incorporated,* presentation at the National Research Council conference on "Science and Engineering Programs: On Target for Women?," Irvine, CA, November 4-5, 1991.

Figure 7-5. Attrition rates at Corning Corporation, 1987-1991, by sex.

- confidential counseling for women, provided by an outside consultant, with general issues reported back to management for review and possible action,
- a new career planning and management system that enables all individuals to exercise more control over their own careers,
- a formalized coaching (mentoring) program primarily for women and minorities to enhance their integration into the corporate culture,
- part-time and flex-time work policies for salaried employees, and
- a required workshop for all RD&E employees that addresses gender-related issues in the workplace.

The Corning workshop has three objectives: (1) to increase awareness and sharpen sensitivity to women's problems in all their subtle variations, (2) to legitimize communications on these subjects, and (3) to help the Technology Group better understand issues of concern to women employees. The basis for the workshop is a video presentation that begins with a message from the vice chairman of Corning pointing out not the ethics of equal treatment of the sexes but, rather, the pragmatic purpose—that is, the company must create an environment where everyone can contribute to his or her maximum capability. The remaining portion of the video, featuring professional actors, illustrates some negative experiences of women in RD&E and forms the basis for discussion in the workshops. Everyone in the RD&E organization attended a workshop session in the first quarter of 1990. People who had made insensitive remarks thus found themselves sitting in the workshops, surrounded by colleagues, as the remarks were re-enacted on film and then discussed by co-workers. A follow-up study, eight months later, indicated that the video and ensuing discussions were helpful in modifying attitudes (Menger, 1991). Another video/workshop entitled "Valuing Diversity" has been prepared and will be taken by all professionals in the company during 1992.

The coaching or mentoring program has been in existence since 1988 at Corning. Coaches are volunteers—in general, experienced employees from another department. Each pair of coach and coachee is given a one-day preliminary orientation by Human Resources personnel, and coordinators meet individually and collectively with the pairs during early stages of the program. An outside consultant was also available during the first year of the program to help the coaches cope with new problems they may not have had to face previously. The pairs meet on a regular basis to discuss work-related issues. The enthusiasm of the first pairs in the program led to extension of the program to other parts of the corporation.

Approximately 40 percent of Corning employees have requested flex-time. As a result,

> The company plans to start "flexibility training" to help managers administer flexible scheduling fairly, and stresses flexibility in career planning as well. Instead of routinely promoting people who follow a traditional career path, including certain transfers and promotions, the focus is on matching an employee's skills, interests and ability to learn with the demands of the job (Shellenbarger, 1992).

At the R&D headquarters, flex-time is granted to all professionals, although all employees are expected to be at the site from 9:00 a.m. to 3:00 p.m. In addition,

> A 17-member Corning task force, ranging from vice presidents to engineers, has been looking for ways to help women advance. One idea: Make part-time work and other family policies explicitly available for reasons that have nothing to do with motherhood, such as a need to spend time with an ailing parent. "Work-family [conflict] must be an employee issue, not just a women's issue," says Marie McKee, Corning's vice president, strategic staffing. (Shellenbarger, 1992)

Part-time jobs are arranged by negotiation between employee and manager. Allowing for part-time work in this time of rapid development of science and technology may be key to attracting and retaining women in the technical ranks. Of those who have opted for part-time positions for personal reasons, more than two-thirds are women (Menger, 1991).

Corning addresses the "glass ceiling" through three mechanisms: (1) early identification of high-potential women and minorities, (2) assignment of responsibility to supervisors for providing job opportunities to identified employees within a specified time (job-switching between divisions, for example, is encouraged), and (3) through detailed annual performance appraisals requiring supervisors to prepare adequately for career development discussions with the employee during the appraisal (Solomon, 1990). By 1991 the attrition rate of women at Corning had decreased by more than a factor of 3, down to less than 5 percent, and is now close to the attrition rate for men.

Xerox Corporation

Xerox is well known for its successful recruitment of blacks in the 1970s and 1980s. This was accomplished by a combination of strong commitment on the part of top management, including setting goals for minority hiring and promotion and establishing minority self-help groups (Graham, 1991). Xerox's Vice-President for Research has recently announced his intention to make Xerox research laboratories the "employer of choice" for technical women. To that end, in 1990, the vice president established a

Women's Council, consisting of six women (two from each of the three Xerox laboratories) to advise him. One of the major goals is to increase the number of women in the laboratories; only 19 percent of the company's research lab employees are female, although the overall Xerox work force is 32.3 percent female. Subsequently, the Vice-President for Research has announced that 50 percent of all new professional hires in the Research Labs should be women.

Company-wide, Xerox has developed a "Balanced Work Force Strategy," a system of calculated numerical targets for all employee groups in all job categories, levels, functional areas and operating units. All group managers are held accountable for achieving balance in their organizations. Balanced Work Force Goals are generated using internal as well as external labor data. Qualified employees are identified, developed and promoted, and operating groups are assessed regularly on the basis of their performance (Catalyst, 1991a).

Furthermore, Xerox managers are urged to "stress results rather than time spent in the office [and] to work with employees as individuals" (Shellenbarger, 1992). According to Patricia Nazemetz, director of benefits at Xerox Corporation,

> We don't assume someone has to put in a 60-hour workweek just because a predecessor took 60 hours to do the job. . . . Managers have to be sensitive to the fact that everyone has a different personal agenda. If a person says, "I can do the job, but I want to do it in four days or by spending part of my time at home," we encourage them to listen to that, and not say, "I have to treat you exactly like I treat Harry. Harry's here 80 hours and you should be here 80 hours too." (Shellenbarger, 1992)

This policy has been beneficial to both female and male employees, but has particular relevance to women, who in general continue to bear most family-related responsibilities in U.S. society.

As a result of the implementation of these policies, the number of women in management at Xerox has increased dramatically during the past years. Among the company's 250 top management positions, 30 are held by women; this contrasts with only 2 women in those positions in 1988 (Shellenbarger, 1992).

Other Corporate Initiatives

According to its 1990 report, *Equal Opportunity at Bristol-Myers Squibb Company,*

> Bristol-Myers Squibb Company believes its commitment to Equal Employment Opportunity is more than a legal and moral necessity: Realizing the potential of every individual is also sound business.

With that premise, the company has developed several programs for recruiting and retaining women and minorities. *Recruitment* programs include summer internships for outstanding women and minority undergraduate students; engineering co-op programs to give mechanical and industrial engineering students experience in biomedical, research, industrial, and development engineering; scholarships for women and minorities in engineering, science, and computer science; and participation in meetings of professional organizations such as the National Society of Black Engineers, Student National Pharmaceutical Association, Society of Women Engineers, and American Indian Science and Engineering Society.

Retention of its highly qualified S&E work force is also important to Bristol-Myers Squibb, and its divisions offer various programs to foster "upward mobility for its minority and women employees." Four of these initiatives are considered especially significant in the company's ability to have a high retention rate for its scientists and engineers:

- *training for company managers:* Sensitizing managers in all Bristol-Myers Squibb U.S. divisions to affirmative action and equal opportunity requirements is directed by the Corporate Equal Opportunity Affairs Department, whose regular evaluations include formal reviews with division presidents.

- *tuition aid:* Programs are in place to assist minority and women employees in obtaining advanced degrees in order to rise within the corporate structure.

- *career development:* The company encourages women to seek nontraditional jobs, to strengthen their managerial skills, and to prepare for advancement opportunities. Courses, conferences, and seminars for employees are conducted by the company's Career Development Center and by Squibb College, part of the Bristol-Myers Squibb Pharmaceutical Group.

132

- *child-care assistance:* The company's U.S. divisions support a variety of day-care programs, such as a referral source that matches parents with appropriate child-care services, subsidized child care at local facilities, and the Family Sensitive Work Environment Task Force established by Clairol, a Bristol-Myers Squibb subsidary, in 1990 "to address opportunities for job-sharing, part-time employment, day care, and flextime."

Among Bristol-Myers Squibb's corporate goals are (1) to seek out minority group members, women, and individuals with disabilities (including Vietnam-era veterans), encouraging them to apply for employment; (2) to ensure that people are considered for employment, training, and promotion solely on the basis of their abilities and potential to perform a job; and (3) to establish the company as a community leader, not only by observing the letter of the law, but also by supporting its spirit and intent. As a result, minorities currently represent 12.4 percent of professional and managerial employees in Bristol-Myers Squibb's U.S. work force, and women represent 33.7 percent—percentages higher than the national averages of 10 and 16 percent, respectively.

Another company taking steps to retain its technical work force is the General Motors Corporation. By means of General Motors Fellowships, the company promotes employee development and retention of talent by offering continuing educational opportunities. Employees pursuing graduate degrees in all engineering disciplines are eligible to apply for these fellowships. The program has been regularly evaluated since its inception in 1978 and, according to program staff, has been shown to be effective in the development and retention of engineering candidates, including women.

Like Bristol-Myers Squibb, Corning, Lotus Development, and other larger companies, Monsanto has instituted sensitivity training as a means for increasing its retention of women and minority employees:

> Monsanto employees take courses that involve lengthy discussion, for a day or so at a time, of their own attitudes to sex and race. By making people articulate their feelings, subconscious bias is brought into the open and—the firm hopes—will be reduced (*The Economist*, 1992).

Other companies taking steps to recruit and retain their women scientists and engineers are regularly assisted and recognized by Catalyst, a New York-based firm whose literature emphasizes its activities "to help senior managers and human resource professionals recruit, develop, and retain management women at every level." Among those corporations honored for their achievements in this area are the following:

- Hewlett-Packard: Its annual Technical Women's Conference focuses on "the achievements of women, . . . communication among women, . . . their awareness of cross-functional opportunities, and . . . [the importance of] role models and mentors" (Catalyst, 1992a). According to Hewlett-Packard's president and CEO, John A. Young, the company "expects the Technical Women's Conference will result in improved recruitment and retention of experienced technical women."

- SC Johnson Wax: Among the several programs "designed to attract and retain the best and the brightest [and] to help ensure that qualified women receive adequate promotional consideration" are internal promotion policies, ongoing training and development, mentoring programs, and tuition reimbursement for graduate studies (Catalyst, 1991b).

- Tenneco Inc: Led by CEO James L. Ketelsen, Tenneco has implemented "an integrated approach that both encourages the recruitment and promotion of women and provides the support network of benefits that help women achieve their own potential" (Catalyst, 1991b). Like many other companies during the past five years, Tenneco has established a Women's Advisory Council, a Work/Family Support Program, and executive incentive program whereby managers' bonuses are based, in part, on the degree to which they achieve Tenneco's goals "for advancing women and minorities."

A recent (1992b) Catalyst study of women engineers employed in industry highlights initiatives at 28 companies. Among those programs are the Management Intern Program of Consolidated Edison, designed "to develop its future managers," and General Electric's child-care referral system, part-time work policy, and unpaid parental leave. In both 1987 and 1990, Catalyst

(1988, 1991b) highlighted the programs of several companies to assist employees in balancing their work and family obligations:

Company	Program
Eastman Kodak Company	Work and Family Programs
John Hancock Financial Services	Innovative Family Care Initiatives
US Sprint Communications Company	An Integrated Approach to Managing Career and Family
IBM	Elder Care Referral Service, National Child Care Referral Service

Evaluation of Interventions

Conference participants considered the characteristics listed on page 124 to be features of good programs. It emerged very clearly in the Irvine conference discussions that the treatment of women at Hughes, Corning, and Xerox—and the measures these companies have taken to recruit and retain women—may not be typical in industry, not even in large companies. It was suggested that both the best and the worst programs for women are found in industry, with academe and government programs somewhere in between. A particular point was made that even if a company has a part-time employment option, it may be "political suicide" for individual women to choose this option.

Evaluation of any intervention requires keeping statistics on the numbers of women in the various ranks, categorized according to length of service, productivity, salary, etc. Attitude surveys are also useful, as suggested in the information given above. Corning has been particularly forthcoming in supplying information on its initiatives in this area; it is not to be expected that many other companies would match this.

Future Directions

Interventions to recruit and retain women scientists and engineers in

135

industry are being implemented in small numbers throughout the country. However, to achieve a level of women's participation in industrial employment comparable to that in the academic and government sectors requires a more directed program of strategic and sustained efforts developed jointly by women scientists and engineers and the companies for which they work. Specifically, four suggestions are offered to guide future direction of such programs:

1   Women should be given incentives to seek employment in industry.

It is likely that a major reason for their low rate of employment in industry is that women have tended rather to look for jobs in academe. This is no doubt dictated by the greater familiarity with the academic environment and the more obvious flexibility in hours and working conditions, desirable for raising a family. The corporate examples of this chapter show that there are industrial employers who allow considerable flexibility and emphasize equitable treatment with respect to pay, promotion, and access to these flexible arrangements. According to anecdotal evidence, still greater flexibility can be found, particularly in jobs where there is not daily pressure for production. There have certainly been instances of paid and unpaid leaves of many months' duration with the same job guaranteed on return. Such arrangements are more likely, of course, for valued employees.

Still another incentive is the personal involvement of chief executive officers (CEOs) in the development of recruitment and retention interventions. Such involvement communicates a "corporate commitment" to increasing the employment of women and minorities. The 1991 Department of Labor study found that:

> With the strong support of the CEO and other corporate officers, [one large defense contractor] has determined to aggressively recruit minorities and women through external recruitment efforts, including executive searches; make "deputy" assignments, when possible, using these positions as training grounds for developing minorities and women as "high potential" managers; encourage executive mentoring and sponsoring high potential or high performing minority or female managers and professionals; increase executive accountability and responsibility for cultural changes at every level through a creative incentive compensation plan.

136

Another company, again with the CEO's personal involvement, has developed monitoring programs to measure the corporation's personnel development, retention and advancement efforts. As a long-term goal, the company is committed to minority and female participation in officer ranks in the same proportion as their participation in lower management ranks. To meet this goal, assignments, educational opportunities, and evaluations are carefully monitored throughout management. High potential minorities and women are identified early in their careers and tracked to assure they are given the same opportunities for development as their peers.

2   **Women should band together in self-help groups within their companies.**

It emerged from the discussion that one of the two essential ingredients of a successful intervention is self-help. (It is not possible to specify a procedure for obtaining the other essential ingredient—top corporate support—but in at least one of the examples cited, its achievement was preceded by, and at least partly due to, establishment of a self-help group.) Models of self-help groups are provided by the black caucuses that operate at Xerox and AT&T Bell Labs. At Xerox, the group maintained close contacts across organizational boundaries, agreed not to compete with each other, and ignored status hierarchies in their efforts to help each other. They held developmental workshops on evenings and weekends and coached each other (Graham, 1991). These efforts not only improved skills and performance levels throughout the group, but helped to overcome some of the built-in organizational barriers to learning that affect people of all kinds in large organizations. Female professional groups could, in addition, be involved in corporate discussions of family benefit options and solutions to dependent-care problems.

3   **Companies should allow maximum flexibility in working conditions and benefits consistent with getting the job done well.**

Although greater flexibility may entail some complications and additional expense, particularly in the case of professional employees, it should more than pay for itself in productivity and company loyalty. Flexibility in benefits, the "cafeteria style" now available at some companies, would also be valuable.

4   To increase the number of women gaining industrial employment in science and engineering, companies should expand the universe from which they recruit entry-level employees.

Although research indicates that women's colleges and Historically Black Colleges and Universities (HBCUs) are highly successful in graduating women with undergraduate degrees in the sciences (U.S. Congress, 1988), on-site recruitment by industry on the campuses of these institutions, particularly women's colleges, is limited. In addition, it has been reported that some major companies limit their recruitment efforts to a few departments at a few universities. As the need to tap the broader S&E talent pool intensifies, companies should undertake steps to diversify their work forces by engaging in recruitment at a variety of higher education institutions.

The measures recommended may have only marginal effects toward increasing the number of positions filled by women in the present state of the economy (summer 1992). However, these measures can make the technical environment a more hospitable workplace for women and enhance both recruitment and retention rates. And, finally, improvements in the work environment for women are very likely to lead to improvements for men also.

REFERENCES

Bristol-Myers Squibb. 1990. *Equal Opportunity at Bristol-Myers Squibb Company.* New York: Bristol-Myers Squibb.

Catalyst. 1988. *Managing Work Force Diversity.* New York: Catalyst.

_____. 1991a. *Women in Corporate Management: Results of a Catalyst Survey and Model Programs for Development and Mobility, Executive Summary.* New York: Catalyst.

_____. 1991b. *The Catalyst Award: Honoring Corporate Initiatives to Promote Women's Leadership.* Program for 16th annual awards dinner. New York: Catalyst.

_____. 1992a. *The Catalyst Award: Celebrating Women's Progress and Promise.* Program for 30th anniversary awards dinner. New York: Catalyst.

_____. 1992b. Findings from a study of women in engineering. *Perspective,* May 1992. New York: Catalyst.

Committee on Women in Science and Engineering (CWSE), National Research Council, Office of Scientific and Engineering Personnel. 1991. *Women in Science and Engineering: Increasing Their Numbers in the 1990s (A Statement on Policy and Strategy)*. Washington, DC: National Academy Press.

The Economist. 1992. Women in management. *The Economist* **322**:17-20.

Frownfelter, Dan. 1991. *Hughes Aircraft Company—Objectives and Obstacles*. Presentation at the National Research Council conference on "Science and Engineering Programs: On Target for Women?" Irvine, CA, November 4-5.

Graham, Margaret. 1991. *Initiatives of Xerox Corporation to Retain Its Scientific Work Force*. Presentation at the National Research Council conference on "Science and Engineering Programs: On Target for Women?" Irvine, CA, November 4-5

Menger, Eve L. 1991. *Selected Employee Retention Efforts at Corning Incorporated*. Presentation at the National Research Council conference on "Science and Engineering Programs: On Target for Women?" Irvine, CA, November 4-5.

Shellenbarger, Sue. 1992. Work & family. *The Wall Street Journal*, June 24, p. B1.

Solomon, Charlene Marmer. 1990. Careers under glass. *Personnel Journal* April:96-105.

U. S. Congress, Office of Technology Assessment. 1988. *Educating Scientists and Engineers: Grade School to Grad School* (OTA-SET-377). Washington, DC: U.S. Government Printing Office.

U.S. Department of Labor. 1991. *A Report on the Glass Ceiling Initiative*. Washington, DC: U.S. Government Printing Office.

139

Research chemists Anne Plant and Steven Choquette investigate the optical characteristics of fluorescent molecules in order to increase the specificity and sensitivity of biosensing devices.
(Photo: H. Mark Helfer, NIST)

8

PROMOTING CAREERS
IN THE FEDERAL GOVERNMENT

by Linda Skidmore Dix

Linda Skidmore Dix is the study director for the National Research Council's Committee on Women in Science and Engineering. Prior to her appointment to this position, she served as staff officer for a variety of studies undertaken under the auspices of the National Research Council's Office of Scientific and Engineering Personnel. Among those studies relevant to her current activities are Engineering Labor-Market Adjustments and Education and Employment of Engineers.

As staff officer for the initial phase of the Research Council's study of scientists and engineers employed by federal agencies, she co-edited with study chair, Alan K. Campbell, the report, Recruitment, Retention, and Utilization of Federal Scientists and Engineers (1990), *from which much of the following information is drawn.*

Introduction

Approximately 202,300 social scientists, computer specialists, biological scientists, agricultural scientists, engineers, physical scientists, and mathematical and computer scientists are employed by the federal government in a variety of work-activity classifications, including research, data collection, management, and testing and evaluation. The major employers of federal scientists and engineers are the Department of Defense, Department of Commerce, Department of Agriculture, National Aeronautics and Space Administration, Department of Energy, Department of the Interior, Department of Transportation, and Department of Health and Human Services. Yet, despite the opportunities and variety of employment offered by federal agencies, some people feel that a host of factors negatively affect the agencies' ability to recruit and retain the most capable scientists and engineers (Dix, 1990). Some of those problems can be addressed in various ways (see Table 8-1). However,

TABLE 8-1: Factors Affecting Recruitment and Retention of Scientists and Engineers by Federal Agencies and Possible Solutions to These Problems

Problem Areas	Possible Solutions
◆ Negative perceptions of government employment	Emphasis on "psychic income" such as laboratory's employment reputation, challenging work, unique facilities and equipment; emphasis on educational opportunities available to government employees
◆ Compensation	Non-salary compensation: pay banding,* recruitment bonuses, relocation bonuses, occupation-specific pay scales
◆ Time required to extend offer of employment	Direct-hire authority, simplified hiring procedures, and increased personnel authority for line managers
◆ Difficulty of promotion after reaching GS-12 level	Pay banding
◆ Restricted role of line managers in salary decisions	Flexibility in increasing salary without promoting, increasing personnel authority for line managers, and occupation-specific schedules
◆ Excessive paper work	Direct-hire authority, computer-assisted classifications, and more generic classifications
◆ Questionable tie between pay and performance	Performance appraisals and multiple components of pay increase that are not mutually exclusive, bonuses, and awards
◆ Personnel ceilings and reductions-in-force (RIFs)	Using adjunct personnel, such as postdocs, flexibility in taking into consideration things other than seniority, simplified classification systems that enable the labs to retrain RIFed staff

* Bands of salary, as opposed to the Civil Service's grades, give wider latitude to managers determining salaries for either entry-level or experienced employees.

SOURCE: Sheldon B. Clark, Differences in recruitment, retention, and utilization processes: A comparison of traditionally operated federal laboratories, M&O facilities, and demonstration projects, in Alan K. Campbell and Linda S. Dix (eds.), *Recruitment, Retention, and Utilization of Federal Scientists and Engineers,* Washington, DC: National Academy Press, 1990.

Efforts to manage the federal work force today must operate in an environment that is significantly different from 20 years ago. . . . Shifting demographics, the rapidly changing international climate, and the declining image of federal employment all argue for some fundamental shifts in the way federal personnel management is carried out. This may be especially true as the government struggles to recruit, motivate, and retain a large cadre of well-qualified engineers and scientists (Palguta, 1990).

Compounding the effects of negative perceptions of federal employment is the fact that women and minorities have not been prime targets of past recruitment efforts, although their increasing numbers in the U.S. talent pool generally make them a viable source of our future technical work force. While employment of women and minorities by federal agencies almost doubled during the 1977-1987 period, only 10 percent of the S&E Ph.D.s employed by the federal government in 1987 were women (White House, 1989). Across all degree levels, the employment of women scientists and engineers by the federal government varies by discipline, from a low of 3.0 percent in agronomy to 50.5 percent in sociology. But, in general, the rate of employment of women scientists and engineers is much lower than that of men (Figure 8-1; CWSE, 1991). However, OPM data indicate larger percentages of women in trainee positions in some occupations—engineering (25 percent), physical science (34 percent), and mathematics and statistics (46 percent)—and increased percentages of women hired in these occupations by federal agencies during the past three fiscal years (Gowing, 1991).

Initiatives of the Office of Personnel Management

The U.S. Office of Personnel Management (OPM), established as the successor of the U.S. Civil Service Commission with the passage of the Civil Service Reform Act of 1978, has undertaken several initiatives to assist in the successful recruitment of individuals to federal agencies.[1] Some of those efforts are described below.

---

[1] Much information for this section was provided by Marilyn K. Gowing, *op. cit.*

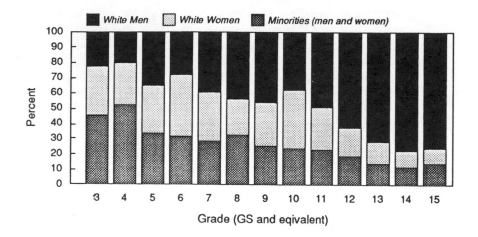

SOURCE: U.S. General Accounting Office, *Federal Affirmative Employment: Status of Women and Minority Representation in the Federal Workforce* (GAO/T-GGD-92-2), Washington, DC: GAO, 1992.

Figure 8-1. Distribution of work force in key jobs for 25 executive agencies, by grade, as of September 30, 1990.

Federal Career Fairs

In March 1990 OPM organized job fairs in Washington, DC; Boston; Chicago; Denver; and San Francisco. Their purpose was to alert the public to the kinds of jobs available in the federal government and to enable federal agencies to publicize the type of work that they perform. As a result of this series of 2-day activities, approximately 87,000 individuals applied for federal positions. Since March of 1990, there have been four Federal Career Fairs for scientists and engineers. The dates and pertinent information regarding each are listed in Table 8-2.

Career America

Developed by OPM's Office of Affirmative Recruiting and Employment, a series of professionally designed brochures describes employment opportunities within federal agencies. In addition, a series of

TABLE 8-2: Federal Career Fairs, 1990-1991

Date	Number of Participating Agencies	Number of Attendees	Number Selected
June 22-23, 1990	63	20,000	888
January 28-29, 1991	66	25,000	812
July 26-27, 1991	56	18,000	670
December 4-5, 1991	68	15,000	249

SOURCE: Marilyn Gowing, *Promoting Careers in Federal Government*, paper presented at the National Research Council conference, "Science and Engineering Programs: On Target for Women?," Irvine, CA, November 4-5, 1991.

videotapes has been created to "enhance the image of Federal service with the 'MTV [Music Television] generation'" (Gowing, 1991).

Career Hotline

Because many students do not know where they might apply and how to find a federal job, in September 1989 OPM set up a college hotline. By calling 1-912-757-3000 and answering a series of questions about one's specialties, degrees, and college(s) attended, a person learns how to apply for a job and is sent the appropriate federal forms for applying. A pre-recorded voice explains the process and the basics of the system.

Automated Applicant Referral System (AARS)

For some shortage occupations, OPM has replaced the SF-171 with an automated form processed within 24 hours at its Macon, Georgia, facility. The rest is left up to the individual agencies. For example, if an agency wants to recruit an engineer, it uses a specific code to hook into this automated system; after specifying the series, grade, and specialty wanted, within 13 minutes the agency will receive a referral of candidates who qualify for that job.

Recruiter Training

OPM has developed a 2-day course, "Recruiter's Interviewing Techniques," to begin in the fall of 1992. When the training becomes available, it will be announced through the Regional Training Centers and the Office of Personnel Management Training Guide. In addition, all Personnel Directors will be contacted and informed of the program.

Federal Occupational Career Information System (FOCIS)

An automated career information system, FOCIS can be used by individuals to assess their skills and interests and then, based on their college majors and scores on the skills assessment, to determine the federal occupations for which they are qualified. In addition, FOCIS contains a listing of federal job openings and the addresses of 1,500 federal personnel offices.

Flexible Benefits

Policies enacted to retain all federal workers tend to benefit federally employed scientists and engineers, both men and women: these include a generous leave program (including leave for parental and family responsibilities), comprehensive health benefits, flexible and compressed work schedules, part-time employment and job sharing, employee assistance programs, dependent care referral programs, and child care centers (OPM, 1988).

In addition to initiatives aimed at recruitment and retention of federal workers in general, other programs implemented by OPM to enhance recruitment and retention of scientists and engineers by federal agencies include flexible examining procedures, direct-hire authority, and special salary rates.[2]

---

[2] OPM, the central management agency within the federal government, has a broad mandate "to exercise leadership in Federal personnel administration. . . to concentrate its efforts on planning and administering an effective Governmentwide program of personnel management. . . to see that agencies are performing properly under civil service laws, regulations, and delegated authorities. . . OPM will have the opportunity for innovative planning for the future needs of the Federal work force, executive and employee development, and pilot projects to test the efficacy of various administration practices" ("Legislative History of the Civil Service Reform Act

Flexible Examining Procedures

The Civil Service Reform Act authorized OPM to delegate examining authority to individual federal agencies. According to the U.S. Merit Systems Protection Board (MSPB), "OPM is delegating examining and hiring authorities to agencies at an accelerated rate and for a wider range of positions than previously. . . . 534 delegated examinations are in effect" (MSPB, 1989a).

Direct-Hire Authority[3]

If individuals are qualified and agencies are satisfied with their qualifications, OPM has authorized agencies to hire those individuals directly. As a result of decentralization, 95 percent of scientists and engineers (essentially, all of the engineers, "hard" scientists, medical specialists, mathematicians, and computer scientists in the federal government) are employed through direct-hire authority—that is, the agencies find potential employees and hire them on the spot in order not to find themselves in the situation whereby desired individuals have taken employment elsewhere.[4] More widely implemented by OPM since July 1989, these changes appear to offer increased opportunities to hire entry-level candidates and may afford agencies a more competitive position in the college recruitment arena.

Special Salary Rates

In addition, OPM has instituted special salaries for scientists and

---

of 1978," House Committee on Post Office and Civil Service, Committee Print No. 96-2, 96th Congress, 1st session (1979), p. 1470).

[3] According to OPM, "direct hire is based on the assumption that the limited supply of applicants and high demand for them assures that all qualified applicants will receive equivalent consideration with or without normal procedures. As an added refinement, direct hire is authorized only for applicants with numerical ratings above a predetermined score (PDS) when there are adequate numbers of basically qualified candidates but few well qualified ones" (*Federal Staffing Digest*, vol. 2, no. 2, Winter 1990, p. 5).

[4] Agencies must rate and rank candidates if more than three apply.

engineers in some shortage occupations. Special rates can be granted based on occupation, grade, and geographic location.[5]

Training and Development

Besides interventions targeted to scientists and engineers in general, several OPM-sponsored, government-wide leadership programs provide for development of *women scientists and engineers:*

- <u>Women's Executive Leadership Program:</u> This program is designed to provide both formal and informal training as preparation for future opportunities in federal management. Of the women high-potential nonsupervisory employees participating each year since this program began in 1984, about 15 percent are scientists and engineers.
- <u>Executive Potential Program:</u> Over 50 percent of the enrollees in this program designed for scientific and technical specialists moving into management are women.
- <u>Legis Fellows Program:</u> Participants in this program receive special assignments in congressional offices and attend congressional briefings and seminars as part of their management training. About one-third of the participants are women, of whom half are scientists and engineers.

Increasingly important to women are "training and development initiatives in the federal government, among the most powerful interventions available in the federal government for retaining highly skilled workers" (Budd, 1991). Numerous studies have documented the increased requirements for scientists and engineers in the federal government, the increasing number of women entering the U.S. work force, and the increased "economic importance of human resource development," according to Budd. OPM has addressed these work force trends through the creation of a set of Human Resources Development Policy Initiatives in three major areas: (1) agency management of human resources development, (2) career development of federal employees, and (3) supervisory, managerial, and executive

---

[5] A detailed listing of these special rates is found in Table 10, *Recruitment, Retention, and Utilization of Federal Scientists and Engineers* (Alan K. Campbell and Linda S. Dix, eds.), Washington, DC: National Academy Press, 1990.

development. Through these initiatives, OPM is directing agencies to develop long-term strategic plans for human resource development and to prioritize training investments to meet true organizational, mission-related needs.

Agency-Specific Initiatives

Speaking to participants at the CWSE-sponsored conference at Irvine in 1991, Marjorie L. Budd, chief of the policy and curriculum initiatives division in OPM's Office of Employee Development Policy and Programs, emphasized five "cross-cutting characteristics of successful programs in the federal government":

1   The programs are part of an organization's strategic business plan, designed specifically by the agency to meet its mission and goals,
2   Scientific leadership and human resources leadership are involved,
3   Programs are developed to create career paths and to prepare routes for women and minorities to rise in the organization,
4   Programs are located in areas of critical need where project work creates a sense of accomplishment, and
5   Flexibilities are built in to provide for two-career families and domestic considerations (Budd, 1991).

Each federal organization employing scientists and engineers has a responsibility to pursue initiatives that will enhance its recruitment, retention, and utilization of that work force. Some agencies have undertaken a vigorous recruitment strategy, recognizing that recruitment is a significant part of a manager's responsibility. Some attempt to reach more potential employees by increasing the number and types of college campuses visited, no longer concentrating their efforts at the major research universities but pursuing candidates at other institutions such as the Historically Black Colleges and Universities (HBCUs). Another recruitment activity is the Career Day held at NASA's Goddard Space Flight Center, designed specifically to show promising college seniors the diversity of work performed by Goddard's scientists and engineers. The results were job offers to more than half of the 45 participants, with over 75 percent accepted (OPM, 1989).

While the aggregate data on retention of scientists and engineers are quite promising—showing that, on average, less than 5 percent leave government employment, about half as resignations and about half as retirements—each agency manager must be concerned within the context of his/her own operation, since turnover varies at the agency level. Some agencies conduct their own research and definition of the problems of turnover by their employees. At least four federal organizations—Naval Research Lab (NRL), Department of Defense (DoD), the Centers for Disease Control (CDC), and the Public Health Service (PHS)—have designed their own data collection systems in order to learn more about their own personnel (Campbell and Dix, 1990).

U.S. Department of Energy

In addition to the many education interventions supported at the precollege and postsecondary levels, the U.S. Department of Energy (DOE) has demonstrated its commitment to the retention of its scientific employees, particularly those who are members of groups that underparticipate in the technical work force. It was stated at the CWSE conference that, "although there had been no programs aimed specifically for women in the Department of Energy, there has been an awareness that women, as well as underrepresented minorities, are an underutilized source for future employment needs in science, mathematics, engineering, and technology" (Verell, 1991).

This awareness led, in 1990, to the first review of programs undertaken by DOE labs to lower the turnover rates of their female scientists and engineers. In the report outline of the DOE program review, it was noted that "to be effective, student education programs designed to encourage young women to enter careers in science and engineering must be accompanied by programs that enhance career development opportunities for those R&D women already pursuing careers in science and engineering. Only by the coupling of these two types of programs will progress be made in the effective and fair utilization of the talents of women in the R&D work force" (DOE, 1990).

The review enabled women scientists and engineers throughout the laboratory system to share their knowledge and experience and to address concerns that permeated many of the labs. The focus was on educational outreach (recruitment) and career advancement of those employed in DOE labs (retention). Participants examined programs implemented at the individual laboratories to help their women employees "who are trying to be successful as scientists" (Bhattacharyya, 1991). During this review it was found that "effective programs for women scientists and engineers employed in DOE laboratories have four major characteristics: they (1) ensure effective

150

recruitment of qualified female candidates, (2) maintain strong networking and mentoring programs, (3) facilitate movement of women into management and senior scientist positions, and (4) encourage the expression and discussion of areas of concern" (DOE, 1990). As a follow-up to the 1990 review, DOE conducted a second examination of laboratory programs for women employees in February 1992.

To recruit and retain the technical work force necessary to fulfill its mandate, Argonne National Laboratory (ANL), operated by the University of Chicago for DOE, has created a standard ladder of career progression. Scientists and engineers are hired at one of eight grades (703-710). Both initial employment and retention are determined by nine criteria related to one's science and engineering education, experience, job-related skills, and work responsibilities (see Table A-6).

A survey of Argonne's practices in employee hiring, promotion, and employee development was commissioned by the ANL director and completed in 1988. The survey not only asked opinions of its 1300 R&D employees on how the lab was doing, but also developed data on what the lab had done as an objective measure of the lab's policies. Among the survey's findings were the following:

- Eight percent of ANL's R&D employees are female.
- Two-thirds of the females are located in 3 of the 23 divisions (biology, chemical technology, and energy and environmental systems).
- Between 1983 and 1988, 355 permanent R&D staff were hired, including 43 percent of the current female staff.
- When both males and females were interviewed for a given position (24 out of 150 evaluated positions), about half of those hired were women (Bhattacharyya, 1991).

Based on this survey, areas of action were identified with respect to recruitment, retention, promotion, management positions, committee representation, and the importance of networking for R&D women.

The establishment of a Women in Science Program Initiator at ANL gives formal recognition to the lab's Women in Science Program. Financial backing from the office of the ANL director provides visibility and a means for the women in science to have input into the laboratory program. Many parties were interested in the role of the Women in Science Program Initiator—the Affirmative Action Office, the Division of Educational

151

Programs (which was dealing with the outreach programs), the Office of the Director (which was providing funding), and the Office of Human Resources (which was interested in recruitment). According to Maryka Bhattacharyya, the first appointee to this position, her office is involved in educational outreach; recruitment, retention, and upward mobility of ANL's R&D women; identification of funding sources for Women in Science initiatives; and communication regarding the ANL Women in Science program. Measures of the significance of the program are the changes that have been instituted within ANL. These include continued development of an outreach program, including an annual "Science Careers in Search of Women" conference; increased sensitivity of managers due to presentations at meetings of division directors, operation managers, and group leaders in the different divisions; assistance on recruitment, such as helping staff locate viable candidates for a managerial position in nuclear engineering; development of programs promoting upward mobility; and identification of potential funding sources for a proposed re-entry program in waste management and environmental engineering.

Other Federal Agencies

Still other federal agencies have implemented programs targeting both students and employees, potential and current (see Appendix A). For instance, the Department of Defense (DoD) supports a wide variety of programs to attract and retain U.S. citizens to careers in the sciences and engineering, beginning at the precollege level. In addition,

> DoD makes a significant contribution to education in science and technology fields by programs provided for its own employees, who comprise 3% of the national pool of scientists and engineers (FCCSET, 1991).

Some of these programs are listed in Table 8-3.

In addition, the Environmental Protection Agency (EPA) has studied the cultural diversity of its work force to address the impact of the changing demography on its ability to accomplish its mission. At present, women comprise about 48 percent of EPA's total work force but only 25 percent of its S&E work force. However, recognizing that the net new entrants to the total U.S. work force will include more women and ethnic/racial minorities during the next decade, EPA is expanding its efforts both to recruit and to

TABLE 8-3: Some Programs to Provide Job-Related Training for Employees of the U.S. Department of Defense (DoD)

Agency	Program
Air Force	• Full-time training in science and engineering for full-time permanent employees • Career Intern Program
Army Corps of Engineers	• Waterways Experiment Station Graduate Institute
Defense Intelligence Agency	• Full-time Study Program
Defense Mapping Agency	• Off-site educational opportunities
National Security Agency	• Advanced Studies Program • After-Hours College Training • Directed Fellowship/Scholarship Program for full-time permanent employees • Grow Your Own Program to fill agency shortages in fields such as collection operations and telecommunications • Computer Operations Associates Program for employees enrolled in computer science, data processing, or computer operations programs at community colleges
Naval Air Development Center	• Part-time Undergraduate Study Award
Naval Ocean Systems Center	• Undergraduate Academic Program
Naval Research Laboratory	• Edison Memorial Training Program (combined work study)
Naval Weapons Center	• Full-time training in science and engineering for full-time permanent employees

SOURCE: Federal Coordinating Council for Science, Engineering, and Technology (FCCSET), Committee on Education and Human Resources, *By the Year 2000: First in the World*, Washington, DC: Office of Science and Technology Policy, 1991.

153

retain members of these traditionally underrepresented groups in S&E positions (Campbell and Dix, 1990). Additional actions are expected in response to the report of an expert panel convened by EPA administrator William K. Reilly, which found that

> the development and nurturing of human resources are central to improving science at EPA. . . . [Yet] EPA provides insufficient incentives to reward the production of high-quality science (EPA, 1992).

Among the recommendations of that panel are the following:

- EPA should expand the use of career development paths, such as those in place for research scientists. The Agency should establish a separate science career track for individuals in the program offices who have appropriate scientific and technical background and who are regularly involved in providing science advice or reviewing science issues and data for regulatory purposes.
- The Agency [should] expand opportunities for rotations that allow scientists from other organizations to work in EPA's science programs and EPA scientists to participate in the scientific efforts of other organizations. . . . A successful rotation should assist an EPA scientist in obtaining promotions and salary increases.
- EPA should use its reward structure to encourage superior science and science management in the Agency. . . . In addition, EPA should develop competitive compensation packages allotted on the basis of comparison with the best of one's peers.

Programs such as those recommended above could serve as interventions to recruit and retain both women and men.

Many agencies are drawing upon the various programs available throughout the federal government to increase the retention of their S&E work force. Some of these same agencies have developed their own interventions, such as fellowships and scholarships for advanced training of their employees, leadership workshops and seminars, and a variety of benefit

TABLE 8-4: Percentage of Women at GS-5, 14, and 15 in Selected Scientific Occupations, 1991

	General Schedule (GS) of Salaries		
Occupation	GS 5	GS 14	GS 15
General physical science	17.1	8.4	4.7
Chemistry	50.0	14.1	8.5
Operations research	56.3	10.5	8.1
Statistics	47.4	19.9	15.8

SOURCE: Marilyn Gowing, *Promoting Careers in Federal Government,* paper presented at the National Research Council conference, "Science and Engineering Programs: On Target for Women?," Irvine, CA, November 4-5, 1991.

packages to meet individual needs (with options, for example, regarding dependent care, continuing education, and insurance coverage).

The Glass Ceiling

In spite of these interventions and the commitment of OPM to "removing all barriers to the advancement of women and minorities once they have entered the federal work force" (Budd, 1991), women scientists and engineers employed by the federal government tend to encounter a glass ceiling, an invisible barrier that has kept them out of top jobs (see Figure 8-1 and Table 8-4). As noted at the CWSE-sponsored interventions conference,

> At the lower grades (GS 5, 7, 9, and even 11), we have substantially high numbers of women scientists and engineers. However, . . . at the [GS] 14 and 15 levels, the percentage of women drops substantially (Gowing, 1991).

Thus, actions must be taken to reinforce initiatives put into place by both OPM and individual agencies. Conference participants discussed a "glass-cutter" program targeted to federally employed women scientists and engineers and delineated its key elements:

- involvement of and open communication between all levels of staff,
- flexibility in job descriptions,
- delineation of the differences between job description and job performance,
- mentoring by senior executives as well as identification of the career patterns that those executives undertook to gain their current positions,
- continuous monitoring and evaluation of the specific intervention, and
- dissemination of the evaluation results throughout the organization.

Summary

The federal government has begun to be more proactive in its efforts to recruit and retain not only its scientific and engineering work force, but more particularly its employees who are women scientists and engineers. Many of the federal initiatives in this area can be traced to the establishment of the Office of Personnel Management in 1972. However, most have been implemented during the past five years, as attention has been drawn to the changing U.S. demography and its implications for employment policies. Nonetheless, change in the actual percentages of women scientists and engineers employed by federal agencies comes slowly, especially at the higher levels of the General Schedule of Salaries, partly because of the low turnover among members of the existing federal work force (MSPB, 1989b). It is heartening, though, to learn that some federal agencies are setting examples for their counterparts by addressing the situation and creating programs to enhance their recruitment and retention of women scientists and engineers.

Future Directions

The report of the National Research Council's Committee on Scientists and Engineers in the Federal Government (Campbell and Dix, 1990) noted two issues regarding recruitment, retention, and utilization that relate to interventions and require further analyses. In particular,

What can be done to enhance federal <u>recruitment</u> of scientists and engineers, especially women and minorities, at the <u>entry level,</u> and <u>retention</u> of scientists and engineers <u>at the midcareer level?</u>

Although not knowing so at the time, conference participants proposed actions in response to that question:

- Assessments, similar to the DOE program reviews, should be undertaken by all federal agencies employing scientists and engineers in order to verify their recruitment and retention rates, particularly of women scientists and engineers; determine the extent to which glass ceilings and walls have become institutionalized; and develop a plan for eliminating barriers to the recruitment and retention of women scientists and engineers within a particular federal agency.
- Drawing on programs implemented in the private sector and in the Department of Energy, federal agencies should design strategies that facilitate networking and mentoring among women scientists and engineers.
- Model programs should no longer function in isolation but should be highlighted as efforts that other agencies might replicate.
- Consideration should be given to the strategy developed by conference participants for counteracting the glass ceilings and glass walls that women scientists and engineers often encounter in the federal government. The proposed process of starting a "glass-cutter program" has five steps:

1   Identify the problem (for example, the number of women in a particular federal agency or laboratory at a given level, when normalized to the actual distribution of women and men in that same category nationwide, should replicate their participation in the overall U.S. work force), gather data that confirms the problem's existence, and identify the audience who will receive and respond to such information.

2   Identify the stakeholders, those who will benefit from changes in policies or programs, and involve them in developing clearly stated goals and strategies for effecting change as well as the rationale for instigating change. Simultaneously, work with

157

others outside the organization, particularly those who have initiated similar programs.

3 Communicate the problem to management, presenting potential solutions and a timeline for achieving them, their benefits, and their costs.

4 Working with management, determine the details of the program to be established.

5 Be patient as the program is implemented and developed, recognizing that only small differences may be noticeable at first and that the "best chance for success includes both 'bottom up' and 'top down' efforts."

REFERENCES

Bhattacharyya, Maryka. 1991. *Focus on the End Point: Quality of Life of Women Scientists.* Paper presented at the National Research Council conference, "Science and Engineering Programs: On Target for Women?," Irvine, CA, November 4-5.

Budd, Marjorie L. 1991. *Training and Development Initiatives in the Federal Government.* Paper presented at the National Research Council conference, "Science and Engineering Programs: On Target for Women?," Irvine, CA, November 4-5.

Campbell, Alan K., and Linda S. Dix (eds.). 1990. *Recruitment, Retention, and Utilization of Federal Scientists and Engineers.* Washington, DC: National Academy Press.

Committee on Women in Science and Engineering. 1991. *Women in Science and Engineering: Increasing Their Numbers in the 1990s (A Statement on Policy and Strategy).* Washington, DC: National Academy Press.

Dix, Linda Skidmore. 1990. Recruitment, retention, and utilization of scientists and engineers in the federal government: Results of a literature review. In Alan K. Campbell and Linda S. Dix (eds.), *Recruitment, Retention, and Utilization of Federal Scientists and Engineers,* Washington, DC: National Academy Press, 1990.

Federal Coordinating Council for Science, Engineering, and Technology, Committee on Education and Human Resources. 1991. *By the Year 2000: First in the World.* Washington, DC: Office of Science and Technology Policy.

Gowing, Marilyn. 1991. *Promoting Careers in Federal Government.* Paper presented at the National Research Council conference, "Science and Engineering Programs: On Target for Women?," Irvine, CA., November 4-5.

National Science Foundation. 1988. *NSF Recruitment of Scientists and Engineers: The Salary Issue.* Paper prepared for the Director and Executive Council. Washington, DC: National Science Foundation, Division of Personnel and Management.

Palguta, John M. 1990. Meeting federal work force needs with regard to scientists and engineers: The role of the U.S. Office of Personnel Management. In Alan K. Campbell and Linda S. Dix (eds.), *Recruitment, Retention, and Utilization of Federal Scientists and Engineers,* Washington, DC: National Academy Press, 1990.

U.S. Department of Energy (DOE). 1990. *Department of Energy Review of Laboratory Programs for Women* (DOE/ER-0510P), November 16. Washington, DC: DOE, Office of Energy Research.

U.S. Environmental Protection Agency (EPA). 1992. *Safeguarding the Future: Credible Science, Credible Decisions* (EPA/600/9-91/050). Report of the Expert Panel on the Role of Science at EPA. Washington, DC: EPA.

U.S. Merit Systems Protection Board (MSPB). 1989a. *U.S. Office of Personnel Management and the Merit System: A Retrospective Assessment.* Washington, DC: MSPB.

_____. 1989b. *Who Is Leaving the Federal Government? An Analysis of Employee Turnover.* Washington, DC: MSPB.

U.S. Office of Personnel Management (OPM). 1988. *Report to the President: Helping Federal Employees Balance Work and Family Life* (OPM Doc. 149-79-9). Washington, DC: OPM. Additional information is available from OPM's Career Entry Group.

_____. *Federal Staffing Digest* 2(1: Fall 1989):7.

Verell, Ruth Ann. 1991. *Programs at the Department of Energy.* Paper presented at the National Research Council conference, "Science and Engineering Programs: On Target for Women?," Irvine, CA., November 4-5.

White House Task Force on Women, Minorities, and the Handicapped in Science and Technology. 1989. *Changing America: The New Face of Science and Technology* (Final Report). Washington, DC: The Task Force.

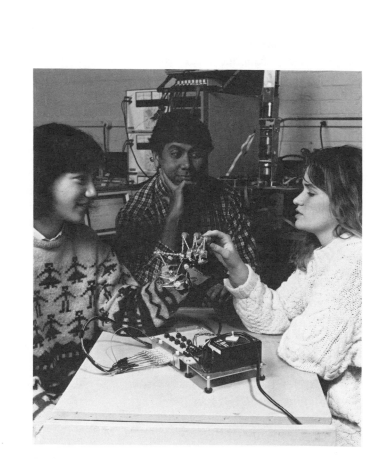

Professor Sunil Singh and two first-year interns in Dartmouth College's Women in Science Project, Dolores Morita and Melissa Downs, work in the robotics lab.
(Photo: Joseph Mehling)

SUMMARY: CROSS-CUTTING ISSUES

Mildred S. Dresselhaus
Linda Skidmore Dix

Dr. Mildred Dresselhaus is an elected member of both the National Academy of Engineering (1974) and the National Academy of Sciences (1985). She is also the Chair of the National Research Council's Committee on Women in Science and Engineering (CWSE) and, in that volunteer capacity, has been the engine behind this enterprise. Her reputation as an Institute professor of electrical engineering and physics at the Massachusetts Institute of Technology and past president of the American Physical Society has helped to push the agenda of enhancing the participation of women in science and engineering to the point that the National Research Council established CWSE in 1991.

Linda Skidmore Dix, study director of CWSE, is an experienced staff officer at the National Research Council, having been responsible for several studies dealing with the education and employment of U.S. scientists and engineers during her 11-year tenure in the Office of Scientific and Engineering Personnel (OSEP) and its predecessor, the Commission on Human Resources.

Introduction

At the start of the Conference on Science and Engineering Programs, Alan Fechter, executive director of OSEP, shared a story about a conference at which Frank Press, president of the National Academy of Sciences and chairman of the National Research Council, was a member of a panel dealing with the question of the vitality of the academic enterprise. At the end of the panel presentation, a member of the audience asked Dr. Press whether there was a shortage or a surplus of scientists and engineers and how supply would affect the vitality of academic institutions. Dr. Press's response was very appropriate in terms of the CWSE conference: "I do not know whether there is an overall shortage or surplus or not. It is a very uncertain enterprise to try to figure these things out. But I do know that we have a shortage of women and we have a shortage of minorities." Mr. Fechter concurred that, whether

161

or not there are shortages overall, the present underrepresentation of women and minorities in science and engineering careers is not to be tolerated and calls for action.

Linda S. Wilson, chair of OSEP, reminded conference participants that there is greater focus on systemic, rather than organizational, change today than in the past. According to Dr. Wilson,

> The systemic focus deals with the whole map, with understanding the system and the ways in which the parts interact with each other rather than in examining just an isolated piece. One cannot look at the whole system without looking at some of the isolated pieces; but in the past we often looked only at isolated pieces and pretended that a system, implicit though it might be, did not exist.

The Interventions Process

Based on both the formal presentations and informal discussions throughout the conference on science and engineering (S&E) programs, a set of progressive actions for implementing interventions, particularly those targeting women, was defined.

Planning an Intervention

While most clearly stated by the Conference groups examining interventions supported by the federal government, the "glass-cutter" program that those groups developed is appropriate for all levels of the education/employment pipeline:

1   Identify the problem, gather data that confirms the existence of a problem, and identify the audience who will receive and respond to such information.
2   Identify the stakeholders, those who will benefit from changes in policies or programs, and involve them in developing clearly stated goals and strategies for effecting change as well as the rationale for instigating change.
3   Communicate the problem to management, presenting details about potential solutions; a timeline for achieving them; their benefits and costs; and a plan for evaluating the program's effectiveness (both

formative/ongoing and summative/end-goal evaluations are essential).

In the process of devising potential solutions, do not operate in a vacuum. For example, although career development seems to be a major component of most S&E education programs, some programs have found that career sessions tend not to be well received and can be eliminated during the first two years of undergraduate study (P. Campbell, 1991). Instead, career development is usually a more effective component in programs targeting college juniors and seniors, who are closer to the time when full-time employment would begin. It should be noted, however, that some interventions—for instance, the University of Washington's Women in Engineering initiative—have been successful in incorporating career development components within their programs targeted to freshmen and sophomores as well as to juniors, seniors, and graduate students.

From the beginning, it is wise to institutionalize programs. Actions of the host institution reveal its commitment to the program and its goals. It is most important that the program fit the institution's "overall aura," according to Suzanne Brainard (1991).

One finding of this Conference was the relatively small number of programs for which evaluation had been built-in at the outset and for which evaluation had been conducted. As a result, determination of a program's effectiveness, particularly whether a program is "on target for women," is most difficult. Research has found that just having a program for women in science and engineering doesn't mean the program will have a positive effect (P. Campbell, 1991). Thus, evaluation must be one component of the intervention, set up during the planning stages of the program. Ongoing evaluation is most important to ensure the effective use of resources and to determine the extent to which the program meets student, faculty, and institutional needs and expectations. For instance, once one has decided to use summer internships as an intervention, one should assess whether students must be kept on campus for the entire summer or whether the programmatic goals might be achieved during a shorter time period.

Funding an Intervention

Programs can be funded solely by a single institution (university, company, federal agency, private foundation) or a consortium of organizations interested in supporting the proposed program's goals. Support by the host institution can be the deciding factor when external sources are considering

163

whether to lend support to a program. Conference participants offered the following suggestions to individuals seeking external funding for their programs:

- Use references such as *The Foundation Directory* to determine those private funding sources that are interested in science and engineering, education, women, and minorities. In preparing a proposal, reveal your knowledge of the foundation's goals and support to activities similar to those you are contemplating.

- Harry Weiner, a program officer of the Alfred P. Sloan Foundation, suggested that communication should not be limited to submission of a formal proposal requesting program support. Instead, he encouraged informal contact, noting that telephone calls are a convenient way to determine rather quickly the extent to which your proposal would mesh with a foundation's goals. Dr. Weiner also emphasized the importance of timing when submitting a proposal: "a bad proposal is one that comes too soon in the life of a program, before the program administrator can point to a successful programmatic outcome, or one that comes up too late as a plea for help after other funding sources have dried up."

- External commitment to an intervention is shown not only by financial support for the program, but also by the personal involvement of corporate and foundation employees in program activities.

- Recognize that available resources are finite and limited. George Campbell, president of the National Action Council for Minorities in Engineering, advised program implementers to "use limited resources intelligently."

Elements of Effective Interventions

From both the formal presentations highlighted in Chapters 4-8 of this report and the more informal discussions among Conference participants, it became apparent that S&E interventions, independent of their level in the education/employment pipeline, shared certain common elements. Among those shared characteristics are the following:

- *an environment conducive to the study or practice of science and engineering*, one in which equal opportunity is provided: As Suzanne

Brainard noted, "One's perception of that environment can determine whether a student pursues study in a particular discipline." She said that her major reason for earning a degree in psychology rather than pursuing a career in the natural sciences, in spite of her interest in math and statistics, was the environment in which math and statistics courses were taught. The environment must permit participants, whether students or employees, to develop confidence in themselves and in their work.

For employed scientists and engineers, a conducive environment also permits job options such as flex-time, part-time employment, job sharing, and even working at home.

- *involvement of the top institutional leaders:* Whether the intervention be education- or employment-oriented, it seldom succeeds for long without the support of top management. As described throughout the earlier chapters of this report, the lack of top support often means the program is "doomed to be short-term, under-financed, and subject to inconsistent resource allocations" (Sposito, Chapter 6). On the other hand, programs having the support of top leadership tend to be more comprehensive in their outreach and effectiveness (see, for instance, Chapter 7).

- *opportunities for program participants to ask questions:* It was pointed out during the conference that a greater willingness to ask questions has been evident among the more successful S&E students, both women and men, at Massachusetts Institute of Technology.

- *peer groups and networking:* Both experienced and newly-enrolled program participants learn from the networking process. In addition to making program participants comfortable with the program, use of peers to help with program operation allows the program administrator and staff needed time to focus on other areas requiring their input. Furthermore, networking with one's peers enables one to "'find out what's going on,' gain political skills, and obtain continual reassurance that the difficulties one faces are not unique or insurmountable" (Sposito, Chapter 6).

- *mentors and role models:* In addition to peer mentoring, such as the Big Sisters program that forms part of the Women in Engineering

Initiative at the University of Washington and other institutions, undergraduate and graduate students benefit from mentoring by S&E faculty and scientists and engineers employed outside academe. In such mentoring programs, noted Suzanne Brainard, "One strategy more important than the identification and matching of mentors and protegees is allowing opportunities for rematching so that both students and mentors can say, 'This is not a good fit. Perhaps something useful can come out of meeting someone else'" (Brainard, 1991).

Mentoring, as shown in the chapters by Conwell and Sposito, is equally important to employed scientists and engineers. Conference participants stressed the role of mentors and role models in "achieving the self-confidence necessary for realizing the goals of any enhancement program" (Sposito, Chapter 6). Mentoring programs should be institution-wide and continuing, not limited to one-shot, isolated efforts.

Precautions

Conference participants experienced in designing and administering S&E interventions suggested several precautions. Among them were the following:

- Don't pursue one large grant for support of an intervention; for when that grant is gone, the program may be forced to end. Instead, conference participants were encouraged to seek small grants from a variety of sources.
- Not all funding sources value innovation as highly as others do. Be sensitive to the organization's previous funding mode, remembering that some foundations are more likely to support a program that has existed long enough to show its effectiveness than to support an entirely new program.
- Be prepared for some less than positive responses to one's plans to target women to participate in interventions in the sciences and engineering. Patricia Campbell (1991) called this the "I don't want to be identified as a woman in science" syndrome, and this phenomenon occurs both for student and faculty participants. She noted that some women students don't want to participate in a program designed especially for women, fearing that their

participation will define them as either in need of remediation or different from other students. Women faculty often feel that they made it on their own and don't see a reason that special efforts are needed for students who have the ability to succeed in science and engineering education and careers.

- Recognize that some negative responses to women scientists and engineers, and to programs targeting them, arise from deeply ingrained cultural biases.   During discussion at the conference, "Science and Engineering Programs: On Target for Women?," Linda Wilson cautioned, "It is especially important for women to recognize that that is true for their male colleagues and that, as we move forward, we need to be sensitive to the adjustments they are making in the way they think and believe about us, just as we are trying to learn about them."

- Interventions targeting women can occasionally have negative effects if inappropriately structured and executed. One example of such a program cited at the conference was a program that emphasized the barriers to being a woman in science: such an emphasis actually discouraged the women program participants from pursuing further studies in science and engineering.

On Target for Women?

In Chapters 4-8 one finds descriptions of a variety of interventions in science and engineering. In addition to those providing financial resources for educational purposes, there are institution efforts to create gender sensitivity (among such programs are training sessions on diversity and incentives and accountability for managers on these issues); women's groups organized to provide a network for women scientists and engineers, both students and employees; assistance with child-care, important both to postsecondary students and practicing scientists and engineers, career counseling and career development programs; and flexible scheduling (classes for students, work hours for employees).

Interventions are important to recruit and retain both women and men in science and engineering. For women they have several purposes, including providing proof that women scientists and engineers do exist, serving as points of contact with others interested in particular disciplines, offering opportunities for career advancement, as well as the development of

167

leadership and managerial skills, recognizing outstanding performance by women, and forming networks that cut across many traditional boundaries. To facilitate the success of a particular effort requires an understanding of the process of implementation, administration, and evaluation. However, the limited duration of many programs and the almost nonexistent evaluation of current programs prevented Conference participants from assessing the extent to which this vast array of interventions is "on target for women." They did, nonetheless, stress the importance of evaluating the effectiveness of all interventions, particularly in light of a number of topics warranting further study:

- Reform of science education at the university level to address retention problems at each level: undergraduate, M.S., and Ph.D.—for example, why do many students who enter doctoral programs in science not complete those programs?

- Cultural and structural discrimination—for example, what must be done to overcome bias that steers females away from careers in science and engineering?

- Public perception of science—for example, what can really change the negative images of scientists and engineers held by many children and adults?

- Student-based systems of learning—for example, what are their impacts on the pursuit of S&E degrees as compared to the influences of teacher-based systems of learning?

- Similarities of underparticipating groups in science and engineering—for instance, what problems faced by minorities are the same as those faced by women?

- Critical mass—by scientific discipline, what level of participation by women, both as students and as faculty, is necessary to ensure an environment conducive to the recruitment and retention of other women in that discipline?

The following comments made by Linda S. Wilson at the conference seem to be an appropriate conclusion to this examination of S&E interventions. When asked whether parity participation of women in the sciences and engineering can be achieved by perturbation theory or by unraveling the current fabric of S&E education and beginning anew, she responded:

168

We will be proceeding more incrementally than by bold
revolution. . . . Nonetheless, these perturbations will
empower men as well as women, and that is what will help
move systemic change along more rapidly. There are many,
many men who have not found the current system conducive
to developing their talents. There are many men who want
just as much as women do to have their children educated
and cared for in a better way. What we are learning is going
to be enormously liberating to the majority of men. What
we are trying to do is to construct good, functional
partnerships with greater understanding. That can be done
with perturbation theory. We do not have to foment
revolution. It does require our continuing to have
confidence and self-esteem and to stay true to our values.

REFERENCES

Bhattacharyya, Maryka. 1991. *Focus on the End Point: Quality of Life of
Women Scientists*. Presentation at the National Research Council
conference on "Science and Engineering Programs: On Target for
Women?" Irvine, CA, November 4-5.

Brainard, Suzanne. 1991. *Mentoring Programs: Using a Generic Intervention
Strategy*. Paper presented at the National Research Council
conference on "Science and Engineering Programs: On Target for
Women?" Irvine, CA, November 4-5.

Campbell, George Jr. 1991. Discussion, *Using Time, Money, and Human
Resources Efficiently and Effectively*. Conference on Science and
Engineering Programs: On Target for Women? Irvine, CA,
November 4 5.

Campbell, Patricia. 1991. *How To Do Everything on Practically Nothing:
Lessons from the Field*. Paper presented at the National Research
Council conference on "Science and Engineering Programs: On
Target for Women?" Irvine, CA, November 4-5.

Nerad, Maresi. 1991. *Using Time, Money, and Human Resources Efficiently
and Effectively in the Case of Women Graduate Students*. Paper
presented at the National Research Council conference on "Science
and Engineering Programs: On Target for Women?" Irvine, CA,
November 4-5.

Weiner, Harry. 1991. *Sloan Foundation Programs Supportive of Women in Science and Engineering.* Presentation at the National Research Council conference on "Science and Engineering Programs: On Target for Women?" Irvine, CA, November 4-5.

APPENDIXES

171

TABLE A-1: Some Sponsors of Postsecondary Science and Engineering
Interventions

SOURCE	HOW TO CONTACT
Akron, University of	Dr. Glenn Atwood Dean, College of Engineering Akron, OH 44325 216-375-7593
American Association of Blacks in Energy	Dr. Leandra Abbott 801 Pennsylvania Ave., SE, Suite 250, Washington, DC 20003 202-547-9378
American Association of Cereal Chemists	Mr. Raymond J. Tarleton, Executive Vice President 3340 Pilot Knob Road, St. Paul, MN 55121 612-454-7250
American Association of Petroleum Geologists (AAPG) Foundation	J. H. Howard, Chairman, AAPG Grants-in-Aid Committee c/o AAPG Headquarters, PO Box 979, Tulsa, OK 74101-0979 918-584-2555
American Association of University Women	Ms. Avis Davis, Program Officer, Educational Foundation 1111 16th Street, NW, Washington, DC 20036 202-728-7614
American Chemical Society (ACS)	Dr. Leroy B. Townsend, Chair, ACS Medicinal Chemistry Division, Fellowship Selection Committee Department of Medicinal Chemistry, College of Pharmacy University of Michigan, Ann Arbor, MI 48109-1065 313-764-7547 Dr. Mary E. Thompson, Chair, Women Chemists Committee 1155 Sixteenth Street, NW, Washington, DC 20036 202-872-4600
American Consulting Engineering Council (ACEC)	ACEC Research and Management Corporation 1-15 15th Street, NW, Suite 802, Washington, DC 20005 202-347-7474
American Economics Association, Committee on the Status of Women	Dr. Elizabeth Hoffman, Chair, CSWEP Department of Economics, University of Arizona, Tucsson, AZ 85721 602-621-6224

173

American Geological Institute	Ms. Marilyn Suiter, Director of Special Programs 4220 King Street, Alexandria, VA 22302-1507 703-379-2480
American Geophysical Union	Director, Membership Programs Division 2000 Florida Avenue, NW, Washington, DC 20009 202-462-6903
American Indian Science & Engineering Society	Mr. Norbert Hill, Executive Director 1085 14th Street, Suite 1056, Boulder, CO 80302 303-492-8658
American Institute of Aeronautics and Astronautics (AIAA)	Director, AIAA Student Programs 370 L'Enfant Promenade, SW, Washington, DC 20024 202-646-7400
American Institute of Physics	Dr. Beverly F. Porter 335 East 45th Street, New York, NY 10017 212-661-9404, ext. 615
American Physical Society	Dr. Bunny Clark Committee on the Status of Women in Physics 335 East 45th Street, New York, NY 10017-3483 212-682-7341
American Psychological Association	Dr. Gwendolyn P. Keita, Director, Women's Programs Office 1200 17th Street, NW, Washington, DC 20036 202-955-7767
American Society for Microbiology	Christina M. Johnson, Office of Public and Scientific Affairs 1325 Massachusetts Avenue, NW, Washington, DC 20005 202-737-3600
American Institute of Chemical Engineers	American Institute of Chemical Engineers 345 E. 47th Street, New York, NY 10017 212-705-7338
American Society for Engineering Education	Dr. Tobi A. Rothman, Director, Women in Engineering Division, School of Engineering & Computer Sciences, California State University, Northridge, CA 91330 818-885-2146
American Society of Naval Engineers	Scholarship Coordinator 1452 Duke Street, Alexandria, VA 22314-3403 703-836-6727

American Sociological Association	Director, Minority Fellowships Program 1722 N Street, NW, Washington, DC 20036 202-955-3410
American Statistical Association (ASA)	Dr. Carolee Bush, ASA/NSF/NIST Research Program 1429 Duke Street, Alexandria, VA 22314-3402 703-684-1221
American Water Works Association	Ms. Kimberly Knox, Manager of Education Programs 6666 West Quincy, Denver, CO 80235 303-794-7711
Argonne National Laboratory	Dr. Robert W. Springer, Director, Division of Educational Programs Dr. John F. Mateja, Program Leader, Division of Educational Programs Dr. Maryka Bhattacharyya, W.I.S. Program Initiator, Bldg. 202 Dr. Norman D. Peterson, Assistant to the Director 9700 South Cass Avenue, DEP 223, Argonne, IL 60439-4835 708-972-3366 or -3923 or -7229
Arizona State University	Dr. Gary D. Keller, Executive Director, Project 1000 Graduate College, Tempe, AZ 85287-1003 602-965-3958
Association for Women in Science	Ms. Catherine J. Didion, Executive Director 1522 K Street, NW, Suite 820, Washington, DC 20005 202-408-0742

AT&T Bell Laboratories   Crawford's Corner Road, Holmdel, NJ 07733-1988
- Special Programs Administrator, Room 1E-209 — 201-949-3728
- Engineering Scholarship Program Administrator, Room 1E-213 — 210-949-4301
- Dual Degree Scholarship Program Administrator — 201-949-5592
- University Relations Summer Program Administrator, Room 1E-231 — 201-949-5592
- Graduate Research Program for Women — 201-949-2943
- Cooperative Research Fellowships — 201-949-2943

- Ph.D. Scholarship Program Dr. C. K. N. Patel, Chair, Technical Relations Committee
  AT&T Bell Laboratories, 600 Mountain Avenue, Room 1A-222, Murray Hill, NJ 07974
  201-582-3425

AT&T Network Systems	Dr. Sheila Pfafflin, District Manager, Human Resources 1 Speedwell Avenue, West, Morristown, NJ 07962 201-898-3452

Augusta College	Dr. Gary Stroebel, Professor of Chemistry Augusta, GA 30910 404-737-1422
Barry Goldwater Scholarship and Excellence in Education Foundation	Mr. Gerald J. Smith, Executive Director, Barry M. Goldwater Foundation 499 S. Capitol St., SW, Ste. 405, Washington, DC 20003-4013 202-755-2312
Bristol-Myers Squibb	Mr. Lionel M. Stevens 345 Park Avenue, New York, NY 10154-0037 212-546-4000
Bureau of the Census w/Bureau of Labor Statistics (BLS), NIST, & NSF	Ms. Carolee Bush, Research Programs, American Statistical Association 1429 Duke Street, Alexandria, VA 22314-3402 703-684-1221
Business & Professional Women's Foundation	Ms. Linda Colvard Dorian, Executive Director 2012 Massachusetts Avenue, NW, Washington, DC 20036 202-293-1200
California State Univ (CSU)	Dr. Costello Brown, Predoctoral Program Director, Office of the Chancellor 400 Golden Shore, Suite 312, Long Beach, CA 90802-4275 213-590-5974
	Dr. Raymond Landis, Dean, School of Engineering and Technology Dr. Margaret Jefferson, Director, Minorities in Science Program 5151 State University Drive, Los Angeles, CA 90032-8500 213-343-4508
CSU-Fresno	Dr. Francisco Pineda, Director Graduate Studies and Research, Fresno, CA 93740-0051 213-590-5974
California, Univ. of	Dr. Ellen Switkes, Office of the President 300 Lakeside Drive, 18th Floor, Oakland, CA 94612 518-987-9479
UC-Berkeley	Office of Women and Graduate Minority Student Programs c/o Carla Trujillo University of California 312 McLaughlin, Berkeley, CA 94720 510-643-6443

Carnegie Mellon Univ.	Dr. Barbara Lazarus, Associate Provost for Academic Projects EDSH 209, Pittsburgh, PA 15213 412-268-6995
CMU Dept. of Engineering & Public Policy	Dr. M. Granger Morgan, Head of the Department Dr. Cliff Davidson, Professor of Civil Engineering Pittsburgh, PA 15213 412-268-2670
Carter Hawley Hale Stores, Inc.	Ms. Jeannette McElwee, Director of Community Affairs 444 S. Flower, Los Angeles, CA 90071 213-239-6905
City University of New York, Queens College	Dr. Burton Tropp, Professor of Chemistry Flushing, NY 11367 718-520-7231
Clare Booth Luce Fund	The Henry Luce Foundation, 111 West 50th Street, New York, NY 10020 212-489-7700
The Coca-Cola Company	Mr. Donald R. Greene, President, The Coca-Cola Foundation PO Drawer 17345, Atlanta, GA 30301 404-676-2680
College of Staten Island, Sunnyside	Dr. Elas Nunez-Wormack, Associate Dean of Faculty 715 Ocean Terrace, Staten Island, NY 10301 718-390-7733
The Cooper Union	Dean of Admissions 41 Cooper Square, New York, NY 10003 212-553-4120
Cornell University	Dr. Michele Fish, Director, Women's Program in Engineering 167 Olin Hall, Ithaca, NY 14853-5201 607-255-3658
Dartmouth College	Dr. Carol B. Muller, Assistant Dean of Engineering 8000 Cummings Hall, Hanover, NH 03755-8000 603-646-3058
Dayton Power & Light Co.	Dr. H. T. Santo, Vice President PO Box 8815, Dayton, OH 45401 513-259-7212

177

Digital Equipment Corp.	Ms. Jane Hamel, Corporate Contributions Program Manager 111 Powdermill Road, Maynard, MA 01754 508-493-9210
Douglass College	Dr. Ellen F. Mappen, Director, Douglass Project for Women in Math, Science, and Engineering P. O. Box 270, New Brunswick, NJ 08903-0270 908-932-9191
East Tennessee State Univ.	Dr. Fred Sauceman, Director, PREP PO Box 24010A, Johnson City, TN 37614 615-929-4317
E. I. DuPont de Nemours & Company	Mr. Stacey J. Mobley, Vice President for External Affairs 1007 Market Street, Wilmington, DE 19898 302-774-8051
Elizabeth City State University	Dr. Sohindar Sachdeve, Director, Departmental Honors Program Campus Box 951, Elizabeth City, NC 27909 919-335-3487
Emerson Electric Company	Ms. Jo A. Harmon, Vice President, Corporate Administration 8000 W. Florissant Ave., St. Louis, MO 63136 314-553-2000
Fluor Corporation	Mr. J. Robert Fluor II, Vice President, Corporate Relations 3333 Michelson, Irving, CA 92730 714-975-7171
General Motors Corporation	Ms. Jenny R. Machak, Director, Placement & College Relations 3044 West Grand Boulevard, Detroit, MI 48202 315-556-3565
Georgia-Pacific Corporation	Dr. W. I. Tamblyn, President PO Box 105605, Atlanta, GA 30348 404-521-4463
Graduate Women in Science	Sigma Delta Epsilon 111 E. Wacker Drive, Suite 200, Chicago, Il 60601-4298 312-616-0800
Hewlett-Packard Company	Director, SEED Program PO Box 10301, Mail Stop 20-AC, Palo Alto, CA 94303-0890 415-857-2092

Holiday Corporation

Ms. Laurisa Sellers, Director of Honywell Foundation
MN 12-5259, Honywell Plaza, Minneapolis, MN 55408
612-870-2368

Illinois State University

Dr. Glen Collier, Associate Professor of Biology
North and South Streets, Normal, IL 61761
309-438-7280

Institute for Industrial
Engineers

Ms. Amanda F. Guthridge, Manager, Member Services
PO Box 6150, Norcross, GA 30091-6150
404-449-0460

International Business
Machines Corporation

Dr. Sadagopan V. Varadachari, Director of Fellowships
PO Box 218, Yorktown Heights, NY 10598
914-945-3000

Iota Sigma Pi

Dr. Linda Munchausen, Department of Chemistry and Physics
Box 372, SE Louisiana University, Hammond, LA 70402
504-549-2160

ITT Corporation

Mr. Juan C. Capello, Senior Vice President & Director of
Corporate Relations, 1330 Avenue of the Americas
New York, NY 10019
212-258-1000

Kerr-Mcgee Corporation

Ms. Paula Davis
PO Box 25861, Oklahoma City, OK 73125
405-270-1313

Lawrence Berkeley
Laboratory

Dr. Martha Krebs, Associate Director, Life Sciences Division
462A Donner Laboratory, 1 Cyclotron Road, Berkeley, CA
94720
510-486-4360

Litton Industries, Inc.

Ms. Nancy L. Thacker, Director of Personnel
360 N. Crescent Dr., Beverly Hills, CA 90210
310-859-3014

Martin Marietta Corporation

Dr. Michael A. Hopp, Director of Management and
Organization Development
6801 Rockledge Dr., Bethesda, MD 20817
301-897-6211

Michigan State Univ.

EOP Fellowship Program, The Graduate School
246 Administration Building, East Lansing, MI 48824
517-355-0300

Mills College	Professor Lenore Blum International Computer Science Institute (ICSI) 1947 Center Street, Suite 600, Berkeley, CA 94748-1105 510-643-9153
Minnesota Mining & Manufacturing Co. (3M)	Mr. Richard E. Hanson, Director of Community Affairs 3M Foundation 3M Center, Bldg 591-30-02, St. Paul, MN 55144-1000 612-733-8335
Minnesota, University of	Dr. Barbara Pillinger, Director, Scholarship Programs 231 Pillsbury Drive, SE, Minneapolis, MN 55455 612-625-0091
	Ms. Kathleen W. Luker, Assistant to the Dean, College of Science and Engineering 10 University Drive, Duluth, MN 55812-9977 1-800-232-1339
Missouri, University of	Director, Women in Engineering Program 204 Rolla Building, Rolla, MO 65401 314-341-4212
	Rover L. Mitchell, Dean, College of Agriculture Agriculture Building 2-69, U of MO, Columbia, MO 65211 314-882-8301
Murray State University	Dr. Gary W. Boggess, Dean, College of Science Murray, KY 42071 502-762-2886
National Action Council for Minorities in Engineering	Dr. George Campbell, Jr., President 3 West 35th Street, New York, NY 10001 212-279-2626
National Aeronautics and Space Administration	Dr. Sherri McGee, University Programs Manager, Office of Human Resources and Education Dr. Robert W. Brown, Director, Educational Affairs Division, Office of External Relations Ms. Margaret Finarelli, Associate Administrator, External Relations NASA Headquarters, 400 Maryland Avenue, SW, Washington, DC 20546 202-358-1524, 453-2171, or 453-8305

National Chicano Council on Higher Education (NCCHE)	Dr. Eloy Rodriguez Director, NCCHE Science Fellowships School of Biological Sciences, T40, University of California, Irvine, CA 92717 714-856-6105
National Consortium for Graduate Degrees for Minorities (GEM)	Dr. Howard G. Adams, Executive Director PO Box 537, Notre Dame, IN 46556 219-287-1097
National Science Foundation	Dr. Joseph Danek, Director, Human Resources Development, Education and Human Resources Directorate Dr. Robert Watson, Director, Undergraduate Science, Engineering, and Mathematics Education Dr. Susan Duby, Director of Fellowships 1800 G Street, NW, Room 1225, Washington, DC 20550 202-357-7552, -9644, or -7536
w/Howard Hughes Medical Institute: at Cornell	Dr. Peter J. Bruns, Division of Biological Science Ithaca, NY 14853-2703 607-355-2376
at Carnegie Mellon	Dr. Barbara Lazarus, Associate Provost for Academic Projects EDSH 209, Pittsburgh, PA 15213 412-268-6995
National Society of Professional Engineers Education Foundation	Ms. Marji Bayers, Director, Professional Engineers in Education & Government 1420 King Street, Alexandria, VA 22314 703-684-2800
New Jersey Institute of Technology	Dr. Jo-Ann R. Raines, Assistant Director, Division of of Cooperative Education University Heights, Newark, NJ 07102 201-596-3250
North Carolina Agricultural and Technical State Univ	Dr. Edward Hayes, Vice Chancellor Greensboro, NC 27411 919-334-7965
North Dakota, University of	Director, INMED 501 N. Columbia Road, Grand Forks, ND 58203 701-777-3037

181

Northwestern University	Dr. Carolyn H. Krulee, Assistant Dean of Undergraduate Affairs Northwestern University, Evanston, IL 60201 708-491-7379
Nuclear Regulatory Commission	Intern Programs Washington, DC 20555 301-492-7000
Oak Ridge Associated Univ	Science/Engineering Education Division PO Box 117, Oak Ridge, TN 37831-0117

- Research Participation Program   615-576-1087
- Faculty Research Program   615-576-3423
- Hazardous Materials Management Training Program   615-576-1090
- Environmental Management Career Opportunities Research Experience   615-576-9278
- Faculty/Student Team Research   615-576-3190
- DOE Programs for Historically Black Colleges & Universities   615-576-3423
- Bureau of Mines (BoM) Academic Program, Science/
  Engineering Education Division   615-576-9655

Oberlin College	Dr. Gloria White, Professor of Mathematics Oberlin, OH 44074 216-775-8466 (or 8384) Executive Director Carolinas-Ohio Science Education Network (COSEN) 314 Samuel Mather, Kenyon College, Gambier, OH 43022 614-427-5825
Office of Personnel Management	Mr. Leonard Klein, Associate Director, Career Entry & Employee Development Group 1900 E Street, NW, Washington, DC 20415 202-606-0800
Optical Society of America	Evelyn A. Roberts, Technical Activities Manager 2010 Massachusetts Avenue, NW, Washington, DC 20036 202-416-1960
Penn State National Space Grant College and Fellowship Program	Dr. Sylvia Stein 101 South Frear, University Park, PA 16802 814-863-7688
Phillips Petroleum Co.	Mr. R. G. Robinson, Director of Community Relations 16 B4 PBJ, Bartlesville, OK 74004 918-661-4597

Potomac Electric Power Co.   Ms. Lorraine M. Drew, Manager, Community Relations and
                             Educational Services
                             RM 506, Washington, DC 20068
                             202-872-3490

Public Service Company of   Evan Spanos, Vice President, Regulatory & Business Policy
New Mexico   c/o Alvarado Square,
                             Albuquerque, NM 87158
                             505-848-2860

Purdue University   Dr. Jane Z. Daniels, Director, Women in Engineering
                             West Lafayette, IN 47907
                             317-494-3889

Reynolds Metals Co.   Ms. Sandra S. Walton, Director, Human Resource
                             Development
                             6603 W. Broad Street, Richmond, VA 23230
                             804-281-2510

San Jose State University   Dr. Joanne Rossi Becker, Professor of Mathematics and
                             Computer Science
                             San Jose, CA 95192
                             408-924-5112

Sandia National   Ms. Denise Robinson, Personnel Division
Laboratories   E. L. Hathaway, Project Manager
                             M. M. Vera, Project Manager
                             J. A. Argyle, Project Manager
                             PO Box 969, Livermore, CA 94551-0969
                             415-294-3371

Sears, Roebuck and Co.   Lori Nipp, Program Manager, Education
                             Sears Tower, Dept 903, 6th Floor, Chicago, IL 60684
                             312-875-4499

Society of Automotive   Ms. Judy Rose, Coordinator of Scholarships
Engineers   Wright State University, Dayton, OH 45435
                             513-873-2321

Society of Exploration   Scholarship Committee, SEG
Geophysicists   PO Box 702740, Tulsa, OK 74170
                             918-493-3516

Society of Women Engineers   Ms. B. J. Harrod, Executive Director
                             345 East 47th Street, Room 305, New York, NY 10017
                             212-705-7459 or -7855

Soil and Water Conservation Society	Director 7515 Northeast Ankeny Road, Ankeny, IA 50021 515-289-2331
Spelman College	Dr. Etta Falconer, Chairperson, Division of Natural Sciences Spelman College, Atlanta, GA 30314 404-681-3643
State University of New York (SUNY)	Director of Minority Access Building T801, State University Plaza, 381 Broadway Street, Albany, NY 12246 518-443-5486
U.S. Dept. of Agriculture	Deputy Administrator, Higher Education Programs Cooperative State Research Service, Administration Building 14th & Independence Ave., SW, Washington, DC 20251-2200 202-447-4423
Farmer's Home Administration	Dr. Jane K. Coulter, Assistant Secretary for Science & Education 14th & Independence Avenue, SW, Room 217W, Washington, DC 20250 202-447-5923
U.S. Dept. of Commerce	Director, Office of Personnel Operations 14th and E Streets, NW, Washington, DC 20230 202-377-2560
National Oceanic & Atmospheric Admin. (NOAA)	Arva J. Jackson, Chief, Educational Affairs Division Universal South, Suite 627, Washington, DC 20235 202-606-4380 NOAA Office of Sea Grant 6010 Executive Boulevard, Rockville, MD 20852 301-443-8886
National Institute of Standards & Technology	Dr. Burton H. Colvin, Director for Academic Affairs A-521 Administration Building, Gaithersburg, MD 20899 301-975-3067
U.S. Dept. of Defense	Chief, Staffing & Support Systems, Directorate for Personnel and Security, Washington Headquarters Services Room 3-B-347, The Pentagon, Washington, DC 20301-1155 202-697-4211

Air Force Office of Research
202-545-6700

Office of Naval
Research (ONR)

Dr. Fred Saalfeld, Director
Ballston Towers #1, 800 N. Quincy Street, Arlington,
VA 22210-5000
703-696-4517 or -4258

Bunting Institute, Radcliffe College
10 Garden Street, Cambridge, MA 02138
617-495-8600

U.S. Dept. of Education

Dr. Donald T. Frazier
MS507 Medical Center, Lexington, KY 40536-0084
606-233-5254

Department of Education, Office of Educational Research
and Improvement
555 New Jersey Avenue, Washington, DC 20208
202-219-2038 or 357-6385

Office of Postsecondary Education
400 Maryland Avenue, SW, Washington, DC 20202
202-708-8391

U.S. Dept. of Energy (DOE)
(see also Oak Ridge
Associated
Universities)

Ms. Cindy Musick, Director, Office of University & Science
Education, DOE, Mail Stop ER-82
Dr. Richard Stephens, Associate Director, University &
Science Education, Office of Energy Research
Mr. Isaiah Sewell, General Engineer, DOE Office of Minority
Impact, Mail Stop MI-1
Office of Management and Administration
1000 Independence Avenue, SW, Washington, DC 20585
202-586-8949, -3547, -5000, or -1593

U.S. Dept. of Health and
Human Services
Centers for Disease
Control & Public Health
Service

Public Health Service Institute, Department of Psychology
Morehouse College
PO Box 121, Atlanta, GA 30314
404-681-2800, ext. 297

Mr. William Murrain
1600 Clifton Road - A50, Atlanta, GA 30333
404-639-3316

National Institutes of Health (NIH)	Dr. Ruth L. Kirchstein, Director, National Institute General Medical Sciences Westwood Building, Room 926, 5333 Westbard Avenue, Bethesda, MD 20892 301-496-5231
U.S. Dept. of the Interior	Office of Policy, Management, & Budget Administration 1800 C Street, NW, Washington, DC 20240 202-208-6182
U.S. Geological Survey	Miss Jane H. Wallace, MPES Program Manager 2646 MIB, 1849 C Street, NW, Washington, DC 20240 202-208-3888 or -6403
	Public Affairs Office, USGS MS 119, National Center, Reston, VA 22092 202-648-4460
Fish and Wildlife Service	Room 3240, Washington, DC 20240 202-208-5634
U.S. Dept. of Justice Drug Enforcement Admin.	Dr. Aaron P. Hatcher, III, Deputy Assistant Administrator, Office of Forensic Sciences, Washington, DC 20537 202-633-1000
Federal Bureau of Investigations	Mr. John Hicks, Assistant Director in Charge, Lab Division Room 3090, 9th & Pennsylvania Ave., NW, Washington, DC 20535 202-324-4410
U.S. Dept. of Transportation	Director of Special Programs, Office for Policy and International Affairs 400 Seventh Street, SW, Washington, DC 20590 202-366-1167
Federal Highway Administration	Mr. Jerry Hawkins, Director of Personnel & Training 400 Seventh Street, SW, Washington, DC 20590 202-366-0530
U.S. Dept. of Veterans Affairs, Veterans Health Services & Research Administration	Dr. Marguerite Hays, ACOS for Research, VA Medical Ctr. 3801 Miranda Avenue, Mail Stop 151, Palo Alto, CA 94304 510-852-5645
	Dr. Elizabeth Short 810 Vermont Ave., NW 20420 202-233-5052

U.S. Environmental Protection Agency	Dr. Sheila Rosenthal, Office of Research & Development Dr. Erich W. Bretthauer, Assistant Administrator, R&D 401 M Street SW, Room 3809, Washington, DC 20460 202-260-7334 or 382-7676
Virginia Commonwealth Univ	Dr. Carolyn Conway, Assistant Professor of Biology 910 West Franklin Street, Richmond, VA 23284 804-257-0100
Washington, University of	Dr. Suzanne G. Brainard, Director, Women in Engineering 10 Wilson Annex, FC-08, Seattle, WA 98195 206-543-4810 Dr. Tekie Mehary, Minority Education Specialist Hughes Biology Mentor Program, KB-15, Seattle, WA 98195 206-543-1942 Ms. W. Cheza Collier Phillips, Program Adviser Office of Minority Affairs, PC-45, Seattle, WA 98195
Western Illinois University	Dr. Harold Hart, Chairman, Department of Physics 900 West Adams Street, Macomb, IL 61455 309-298-1596
Western Kentucky University	Dr. George Vourvopoulos, Professor of Physics Bowling Green, KY 42101 502-745-4357
Westinghouse Electric Corp.	Dr. Cheryl L. Kubelick, Manager, Contribution & Community Affairs 11 Stanwix, Pittsburgh, PA 15222 412-642-6035
Zonta International	Dr. Bonnie Koenig 557 W. Randolph Street, Chicago, IL 60606-2284 312-930-5848

187

TABLE A-2: Some Undergraduate Science and Engineering Interventions in the United States

Program Type	Sponsor	Targeted Group*
Career Planning	Argonne National Lab	Women
	Association for Women in Science	AWIS chapter members
	New Jersey Institute of Technology	Students with GPA of 2.8+
Cooperative Education Programs/Traineeships	E. I. DuPont	
	Environmental Protection Agency	
	Lawrence Berkeley Lab	
	NASA	
	Northwestern University	Minorities w/2.0+ GPA
	Oak Ridge Associated Universities	Sophomores w/3.0+ GPA
	Sandia National Labs	
	U.S. Dept of Commerce + NIST	Physical science, engineering, mathematics, and computer science majors
	U.S. Dept of Energy	HBCUs
	U.S. Dept of the Interior: Geological Survey	
Comprehensive Programs	American Geological Institute	Black, Hispanic, or Native American geoscience students
	California St Univ, Los Angeles	Underrepresented minorities
	California, University of	Women and minorities
	Carolinas-Ohio Science Education Net	Blacks and women
	Cornell University	Women
	Dartmouth College	Women
	Douglass College	Women
	National Action Council for Minorities in Engineering	Minorities in engineering

188

Category	Organization	Eligibility
Educational Assistance to Universities	North Dakota, University of	Native Americans pursuing health-related careers
	Purdue University	Women
	Washington, University of	Women
	U.S. Dept of Energy	HBCUs
	Pennsylvania Space Grant Consortium + Pennsylvania Evaluation Project	Any interested Pennsylvania institution of higher education
Honors Programs	City University of New York, Queens College	Incoming freshmen and sophomores
	Elizabeth City State University	College juniors
	U.S. Dept of Energy	HBCUs
Internships & Part-Time Employment	American Indian Science and Engineering Society	Native Americans interested in careers in science-based disciplines
	Fluor Corporation	Engineering majors
	Oak Ridge Associated Universities	U.S. citizens w/B average; students at HBCUs
	Hewlett-Packard Co.	Women & minorities who are strong academic achievers
	NASA	Minorities
	National Science Foundation	
	Potomac Electric Power	Minorities
Mentoring Programs	Association for Women in Science	AWIS chapter members
	Bristol-Myers Squibb	Women
	California, University of	Women & minorities
	Oberlin College	Women & minorities
	U.S. Dept of Education	Minorities interested in physiology
	Washington, University of	Women and minorities
Scholarships, Fellowships, Grants	American Assoc. of Blacks in Energy	
	American Assoc. of Cereal Chemists	Students interested in cereal or oilseed technology

189

Organization	Eligibility
American Consulting Engineering Council	Juniors, seniors, or 5th-year students
American Indian Science and Engineering Society	American Indians studying science, engineering, medicine, and natural resources management
American Geophysical Union	Students accepted to graduate programs
American Institute of Aeronautics & Astronautics + United Technologies, + Pratt & Whitney	Students completing 1 academic quarter with 3.0 GPA
American Physical Society	Minorities
American Society of Naval Engineers	Full-time students in last 1 or 2 years of degree program
Argonne National Lab	Minorities
AT&T Bell Labs	U.S. citizen minorities and women
Barry M. Goldwater Foundation	Students preparing for careers in mathematics or the natural sciences
Bristol-Myers Squibb	Minorities
Business & Professional Women's Fdn.	Minority women over age 25; within 24 months of graduation; in accredited engineering program
California, University of	Women and minorities
Carter Hawley Hale	Minorities
Clare Booth Luce Fund	Students in physics, chemistry, biology, meteorology, engineering, computer science, and mathematics at specified institutions
Coca-Cola Company	Minorities
The Cooper Union	Those with high SAT and ACT scores
Dayton Power & Light	Women, minorities, and individuals with disabilities
Digital Equipment Corporation	Minorities attending St. Louis Community College
Emerson Electric Company	Seniors at HBCUs
Environmental Protection Agency	Engineering majors
Fluor Corporation	Sophomore engineering majors
General Motors Corporation	
Georgia-Pacific Corporation	
Holiday Corporation	Needy students

Organization	Eligibility
Institute of Industrial Engineers	Full-time student in industrial engineering & active IIE member
International Business Machines Corp	Women and minorities
Iota Sigma Pi	Women
ITT Corporation	Dependents of employees
Kerr-McGee Corporation	Students at University of Oklahoma and Oklahoma State University
Litton Industries, Inc.	Dependents of employees
Martin Marietta Corporation	Students living near corporate facilities
Minnesota Mining & Manufacturing (3M)	Minorities
Minnesota, University of	Freshmen minorities in top 15% of HS graduating class
Missouri, University of	Women of high academic ability
NASA	
National Action Council for Minorities in Engineering	Blacks, Hispanics, and Native Americans
National Chicano Council on Higher Education	Hispanic or Chicano sophomores or juniors
National Society of Professional Engineers Education Foundation	Juniors and seniors interested in nuclear energy
North Carolina A&T	U.S. citizens w/B average;
Oak Ridge Associated Universities students at HBCUs	Minorities
Oberlin College	Minorities
Potomac Electric Power	Oregon residents
Reynolds Metals Co	Students enrolled in ABET-accredited engineering program
Society of Automotive Engineers	Students having financial need and competence
Society of Exploration Geophysicists	Women
Society of Women Engineers	
+ Corning	
Soil and Water Conservation Society	Full-time juniors and seniors
U.S. Dept of Commerce: NOAA	

U.S. Dept of Education	American Indians; students demonstrating outstanding academic achievement
U.S. Dept of Transportation: Federal Highway Administration	
U.S. Dept of Veterans Affairs: Veterans Health Services & Research Administration	Students in final 1-2 years of study
U.S. Environmental Protection Agency	Native Americans interested in careers relating to environmental protection on Indian reservations
Western Kentucky University	High-ability freshmen
Westinghouse Electric	Minorities
Semester Courses and Laboratory Experiences	
Akron, University of	Freshmen in chemical, civil, & electrical engineering
Argonne National Lab	U.S. citizen juniors and seniors w/3.0+ GPA
Augusta College	Chemistry majors
Carnegie Mellon University	Freshman engineering majors; upperclass in other majors
Lawrence Berkeley Lab	Women, minorities, and economically disadvantaged CA community college students transferring to UC-Berkeley
Murray State University	Entering freshmen or transfer students
National Science Foundation + Howard Hughes Medical Institute: Cornell University, Carnegie Mellon	Cornell junior biology majors; particularly women & minorities
Oak Ridge Associated Universities	Varies; U.S. citizens;
Oberlin College	Minorities
U.S. Dept of Energy	
U.S. Dept of Health and Human Services: Centers for Disease Control	Minorities
Virginia Commonwealth University	Biology majors having 3.5+ GPA
Western Illinois University	Freshman physics and pre-engineering majors

	American Assoc. of Blacks in Energy	
Seminars		
Summer Bridge Programs	California St University	New students
Summer Research	Argonne National Lab	U.S. citizens w/3.0+ GPA
	AT&T Bell Labs	U.S. citizens having 3.0+ GPA
	California, University of	Women & minorities
	College of Staten Island, Sunnyside	Advanced undergraduates
	Environmental Protection Agency	Students in Cincinnati and North Carolina
	Fluor Corporation	Engineering majors
	General Motors Corp	Sophomore engineering majors
	Illinois St University	Biology majors
	Lawrence Berkeley Lab	Women and minorities
	Lawrence Livermore National Lab	Upper-division women & minority students pursuing secondary-level teaching credentials in S&E
	Mills College	Women
	Minnesota, University of	
	Minnesota Mining & Manufacturing (3M)	Minorities
	NASA	Minorities
	National Science Foundation + Howard Hughes Medical Institute: Cornell University, Carnegie Mellon	Cornell junior biology majors, particularly women & minorities
	North Dakota, University of	Native Americans preparing to become medical professionals
	Oak Ridge Associated Universities	U.S. citizens w/B average; students at HBCUs
	Oberlin College	Women and minorities
	Potomac Electric Power	
	Sandia National Labs	Minorities
	U.S. Dept of Commerce	Minorities
	U.S. Dept of Energy	

	U.S. Dept of Health and Human Services: Centers for Disease Control, National Institutes of Health	Minority sophomores, juniors, or seniors
	U.S. Dept of the Interior: Geological Survey	Students recommended by National Association of Geology Teachers
	U.S. Dept of Justice + Federal Bureau of Investigations	Upper-level students
Travel Grants	American Chemical Society	Women students presenting research findings at professional meetings
	Association for Women in Science	AWIS chapter members
Tutorial\Academic Workshops	Association for Women in Science	AWIS chapter members
	San Jose State University	Freshmen math and science majors
	Society of Women Engineers	SWE members

* Unless otherwise indicated, the program is open to all undergraduate science and engineering majors.

NOTE: "Minorities" refers to those racial/ethnic groups traditionally underparticipating in science and engineering.

TABLE A-3: Some Graduate and Postdoctoral Science and Engineering Interventions in the United States

Program Type	Sponsor	Targeted Group*
Achievement Awards	American Institute of Aeronautics & Astronautics	MA students in aeronautics and/or astronautics
	Society of Women Engineers	Student member of SWE
Career Development	American Economics Association	Women economists
	American Society for Engineering Education	Women engineering and technology students and faculty
Cooperative Education Programs/Traineeships	AT&T Bell Labs	Women & minorities in full-time S&E programs
	U.S. Dept of Commerce + National Oceanic & Atmospheric Administration	
	U.S. Dept of the Interior: Fish & Wildlife Service	
Comprehensive Programs	American Geological Institute	Black, Hispanic, or Native American geoscience students
	Arizona State University	U.S. Hispanic students
	U.S. Dept of the Interior	Minority & women students pursuing study in geology, remote sensing, and hydrology
	U.S. Dept of Veterans Affairs	Students enrolled in PhD program in specific disciplines
Fellowships & Scholarships & Associateships	American Assoc. of Cereal Chemists	Students in MS or PhD program at institution conducting fundamental studies for the advancement of cereal science & technology
	American Association of University Women	Women completing all required coursework & examinations for PhD

195

Organization	Eligibility
American Chemical Society	Third or fourth-year doctoral student
American Geophysical Union	Women of high academic achievement and promise; 1st-year graduate student
American Indian Science & Engineering Society	American Indians
American Institute of Aeronautics & Astronautics: Liquid Propulsion Technical Cmte, General Aviation Systems Technical Cmte	U.S. citizens in liquid rocket propulsion field, general aviation, with at least 1 academic year complete; GPA = 3.0+
American Institute of Physics	
American Psychological Association	Minorities; neuroscience students
American Society of Chemical Engineers	
American Society for Microbiology	U.S. citizens, minority PhD candidates at accredited school
American Sociological Association	Black, Hispanic, American Indian, and Asian American students
American Water Works Association	
Association for Women Geoscientists Foundation	Women with an interrupted education
Association for Women in Science	Women in life, physical, social science or engineering
AT&T Bell Labs	U.S. citizens, PhD candidates
Bristol-Myers Squibb + The Commonwealth Fund	Minorities
Business & Professional Women's Fdn.	Minority women over age 25
California State University, Fresno	Underrepresented minorities
California, University of	
Carnegie Mellon University	PhD students in civil engineering
Clare Luce Booth Fund	Students in physics, chemistry, biology, meteorology, engineering, computer science, and mathematics
Institute of Industrial Engineers	Full-time industrial engineering & active IIE member; GPA = 3.4+
International Business Machines Corp	

Organization	Eligibility
Michigan State University	Minority U.S. citizens who demonstrate academic ability & financial need
Missouri, University of	U.S. citizens, primarily minorities
NASA	Institutions interested in cooperative inter-disciplinary research between universities, industry, and state and local governments
National Consortium for Graduate Degrees for Minorities	U.S. citizens; racial/ethnic minorities
National Institutes of Health	U.S. citizens; minorities
National Science Foundation	Master's program in Business, Engineering Management, or Public Administration
National Society of Professional Engineers Education Foundation	Black women
Spelman College	New graduate students, graduate students of opportunity programs, and graduate teaching assistants who are racial/ethnic minorities
State University of New York	U.S. citizens having demonstrated academic excellence and a commitment to a career in the food and agricultural sciences
U.S. Dept of Agriculture	Students in marine-related fields showing promise of contribution to NIST programs
U.S. Dept of Commerce: NOAA & NIST	Women PhDs at critical points in their careers
U.S. Dept of Defense	Full-time minorities & women students of exceptional ability and demonstrated financial need
U.S. Dept of Education	U.S. citizens; HBCUs; students of nuclear engineering at University of California
U.S. Dept of Energy	Students with less than 1 year of graduate school
U.S. Dept of the Interior: Bureau of Mines	
U.S. Dept of Veterans Affairs:	HBCUs
U.S. Environmental Protection Agency	Women qualified for graduate study
Zonta International	

Grants & Loans

American Association of Petroleum Geologists	Studies relating to the search & development of hydrocarbons & economic sedimentary minerals and/or to environmental geology
American Association of University Women	Women in PhD programs
Association for Women in Science	AWIS chapter member
Business & Professional Women's Fdn.	U.S. citizens, full or part time women students
California State University	New and continuing full-time students enrolled in doctoral programs at accredited universities
Graduate Women in Science	U.S. and Canadian citizens showing outstanding academic ability and involved in research
NASA	Doctoral candidates in social/behavioral or biological sciences
National Institutes of Health	U.S. citizens, minorities

Internships, Traineeships, & Part-Time Employment

American Psychological Association	U.S. citizens pursuing PhD full time or careers leading to delivery of psychological service or research science
Bristol-Myers Squibb	Women & minorities who are strong academic achievers
Hewlett-Packard Co.	Graduate students & faculty
Lawrence Berkeley Lab	Minorities and women
Minnesota, University of	U.S. citizens currently enrolled in graduate program related to training technology
Oak Ridge Associated Universities	Outstanding students in specific S&E disciplines
Sandia National Labs	
U.S. Dept of Defense	U.S. citizens having B average in applicable fields; degree students in energy-related major
U.S. Dept of Energy	
U.S. Dept of Justice	Well-qualified, upper-level students in biochemistry, chemistry, and physics
U.S. Environmental Protection Agency	Students at HBCUs interested in seeking solutions to major environmental problems
U.S. Geological Survey	Minorities & women

198

Mentoring Programs

Organization	Eligibility
American Economics Association	Women in the economics profession
Association for Women in Science	AWIS chapter member
Bristol-Myers Squibb	Women
California, University of	

Research, Semester Courses, & Laboratory Experiences

Organization	Eligibility
American Psychological Association	U.S. citizens, minority students in full-time doctoral program
American Statistical Association	U.S. citizen juniors and seniors w/3.0+ GPA
Argonne National Lab	Graduate students & faculty
Carnegie Mellon University, Dept. of Engineering & Public Policy	U.S. citizens, full-time students
Lawrence Berkeley Lab	Students in chemistry, biology, or physics at minority institution
NASA	
National Institutes of Health	U.S. citizens, team of 1 student and 1 full-time faculty member at accredited colleges or universities
Oak Ridge Associated Universities	High-ability students in Master's degree programs
Sandia National Labs	Black women
Spelman College	Postdocs in selected S&E fields
U.S. Dept of Defense	U.S. citizens; Master's and PhD candidates; postgrads; recent postgrads with degree in appropriate field
U.S. Dept of Energy	

Summer Research

Organization	Eligibility
AT&T Bell Labs	U.S. citizens, women & minorities having 3.0+ GPA; outstanding BS, MS, and PhD candidates within 2 years of graduation
California State University	Minority, disabled and women students
California State University, Fresno	Underrepresented minorities
East Tennessee State University	Native-born minorities, persons who are disadvantaged socially, educationally, or economically
National Institutes of Health	Students in chemistry, biology, or physics at minority institution

Oak Ridge Associated Universities	U.S. citizens, team of 1 student and 1 full-time faculty member at accredited colleges or universities
Sandia National Labs	High-ability students
Spelman College	Black women
U.S. Dept of Defense	
U.S. Dept of Health and Human Services: Centers for Disease Control and Public Health Service	U.S. citizens, minorities
Travel Grants	
American Chemical Society	Women students presenting research findings at professional meetings
American Physical Society	Women physicists
California, University of, Berkeley	Women and ethnic minorities
Optical Society of America	members of OSA
Tutorial\Academic Workshops	
Argonne National Labs	Women
Lawrence Berkeley Lab	U.S. citizens; minority students & faculty

* Unless otherwise indicated, the program is open to all graduate science and engineering majors.
NOTE: "Minorities" refers to those racial/ethnic groups traditionally underparticipating in science and engineering.

200

TABLE A-4. NRC Research Associateship Programs, 1992 Program Year.

Postdoctoral Research Associateship (Type I) Programs

The Aerospace Corporation	(AERO)
National Institute of Standards & Technology	(NIST)
U.S. Geological Survey	(USGS)

Resident Research Associateship (Type II) Programs

Alcohol, Drug Abuse and Mental Health Administration	(ADAMHA)
Armed Forces Radiobiology Research Institute	(AFRRI)
Federal Highway Administration	(FHWA)
Center for Devices and Radiological Health	(CDRH)
Morgantown Energy Technology Center	(METC)
NASA-Ames Research Center	(ARC)
NASA-Goddard Space Flight Center	(GSFC)
NASA-Jet Propulsion Laboratory	(JPL)
NASA-Johnson (Lyndon B.) Space Center	(JSC)
NASA-Kennedy (John F.) Space Center	(KSC)
NASA-Langley Research Center	(LaRC)
NASA-Lewis Research Center	(LeRC)
NASA-Marshall (George C.) Space Flight Center	(MSFC)
NASA-Science and Technology Laboratory	(STL)
National Center for Infectious Diseases	(NCID)
National Institute for Occupational Safety and Health	(NIOSH)
National Institutes of Health	(NIH)
National Oceanic and Atmospheric Administration	(NOAA)
Naval Command, Control and Ocean Surveillance Center Research, Development, Test, and Evaluation Division	(NRaD)
Naval Medical Research and Development and Command	(NMRDC)
Naval Postgraduate School	(NPS)
U.S. Air Force Laboratories	(USAF)
U.S. Army Armament Research, Development and Engineering Center	(ARDEC)
U.S. Army Ballistic Research Laboratory	(BRL)
U.S. Army Chemical research, Development and Engineering Center	(CRDEC)
U.S. Army Electronics Technology and Devices Lab	(ETDL)
U.S. Army Harry Diamond Laboratories	(HDL)
U.S. Army Medical Research & Development Command	(AMRDC)
U.S. Army Missile Command	(MICOM)
U.S. Army Research Institute for the Behavioral and Social Sciences	(ARI)
Battlefield Environment Directorate	(BED)
U.S. Environmental Protection Agency	(EPA)
U.S. Fish and Wildlife Service	(FWS)

Cooperative Research Associateship (TYPE III) Programs

Naval Research Laboratory	(NRL)

TABLE A-5: Some Interventions to Recruit and Retain Science and Engineering Faculty in the United States

Program Type	Sponsor	Targeted Group*
Achievement & Development Awards	American Chemical Society	Outstanding academic chemists
	American Indian Science & Engineering Society	Outstanding teachers of Native Americans
	American Society for Engineering Education	Outstanding women engineering and engineering technology faculty
	International Business Machines	Non-tenured faculty
	U.S. Dept of the Interior: Bureau of Mines	U.S. citizens, full-time, non-tenured faculty at accredited institutions
	National Science Foundation	Women
	Public Service Company of New Mexico	Faculty at New Mexico's six public universities
	Sears, Roebuck and Co.	Undergraduate faculty
	Society of Women Engineers	Women engineers
Career Development & Advancement	American Society for Engineering Education	Outstanding women engineering and engineering technology faculty
	Lawrence Berkeley Labs	U.S. citizens, minorities and full-time faculty at specified institutions
	National Science Foundation	Women & minority researchers
Comprehensive Programs	California, University of	Women & minorities
	Lawrence Berkeley Labs	Community college faculty in environmental technology
	National Institutes of Health	Faculty & students at institutions with substantial minority enrollments
	U.S. Dept of Energy	Faculty at HBCUs

202

Category	Organization	Eligibility
Equipment	Digital Equipment Corporation	Non-tenured faculty
Fellowships & Scholarships & Associateships	California, University of	Women & minorities
Grants & Loans	Clare Booth Luce Fund National Institutes of Health National Science Foundation	Junior women faculty of the highest calibre Faculty at minority institutions U.S. citizens; women or members of underrepresented minority groups
	Sears, Roebuck and Co.	

Research & Laboratory Experiences	Bureau of the Census:
	    Bureau of Labor Statistics
	    + National Institute of
	      Standards & Technology
	    + National Science Foundation
		Recognized researchers submitting detailed proposals

	Environmental Protection Agency Lawrence Berkeley Labs	Faculty at HBCUs U.S. citizens, team of 1 student & 1 full-time faculty member at accredited institution
	National Science Foundation	Full-time, tenured or tenure-track faculty members; promising minority investigators
	Nuclear Regulatory Commission U.S. Dept of Defense: Office of Naval Research U.S. Dept of Energy	Qualified faculty at HBCUs Academic researchers who have held a Ph.D. for less than 5 years Undergraduate faculty; team of 1 student and 1 full-time faculty member, U.S. citizens, at accredited institutions; faculty at HBCUs; full-time faculty
Sabbaticals	Sandia National Labs + Associated Western Univ	Faculty in science

203

Summer Research

Argonne National Lab — U.S. citizens, full-time faculty at U.S. institutions

NASA

+ American Society for Engineering Education — U.S. citizens with teaching/research aspirations

Oak Ridge Associated Universities — U.S. citizens, full-time, permanent faculty member at accredited U.S. college or university

U.S. Dept of Energy:
Bureau of Engraving & Printing — Full-time faculty at HBCUs, U.S. citizens

Visiting Scientists Programs & Workshops

American Indian Science and Engineering Society — Math and science faculty

American Physical Society — Women physicists in academe

U.S. Dept of Justice:
Federal Bureau of Investigation — Full-time faculty in forensic research, infrared analysis or soil analysis, organic trace analysis

* Unless otherwise indicated, the program is open to all science and engineering faculty.
NOTE: "Minorities" refers to those racial/ethnic groups traditionally underparticipating in science and engineering.

TABLE A-6: Some Interventions o Recruit and Retain Scientists and Engineers in the Federal Work Force

Program Type	Sponsor	Targeted Group*
Career Development	Argonne National Lab Environmental Protection Agency Nuclear Regulatory Commission Office of Personnel Management	All degree levels Women & minorities All NRC employees Nonsupervisory employees; scientific and technical specialists; managers
	U.S. Dept of Agriculture: Farmer's Home Administration	Technical employes at all levels
Continuing Education	Nuclear Regulatory Commission	Engineers
Comprehensive Programs	Argonne National Lab U.S. Dept of Defense: Office of Naval Research U.S. Dept of Energy	Appointment Female postdocs 50% of program participants are in S&E fields
Fellowships & Scholarships & Associateships	Environmental Protection Agency U.S. Dept of Defense U.S. Dept of Health & Human Services	Open to all levels and occupations Recent B.S. recipients Ph.D. employees
Flexplace	U.S. Office of Personnel Management	Current employees engaged in "portable" work and whose most recent performance rating was at least "Fully Successful;" must be able to work without close supervision
Internships, Traineeships, & Part-Time Employment	Nuclear Regulatory Commission	Recent college graduates (entry-level employees) having limited nuclear-related, industrial, and regulatory experience

205

Rotational Assignments	Nuclear Regulatory Commission	All NRC employees
Seminars	NASA	Journey-level women in S&E occupations
Visiting Scientists Programs & Workshops	Argonne National Lab	Women
	Environmental Protection Agency	GS/GM-13-15, PHS commissioned officers, SES

* Unless otherwise indicated, the program is open to all scientists and engineers in the federal government.
NOTE: "Minorities" refers to those racial/ethnic groups traditionally underparticipating in science and engineering.

APPENDIX B

Science and Engineering Programs: On Target for Women?
A Conference
NAS/NAE Beckman Center
November 4-5, 1991

SPEAKERS/PANELISTS

Ms. Pamela H. Atkinson
Director
Televised Instruction in
  Engineering
205 McLaughlin Hall
University of California
Berkeley, CA 94720

Dr. Maryka Bhattacharyya
Women in Science Program
  Initiator
Argonne National Laboratory
9700 South Cass Avenue
Building 202
Argonne, IL 60439-4832

Dr. Stephanie J. Bird
Special Assistant to the Associate
  Provost
77 Massachusetts Avenue, 12-187
Cambridge, MA 02139

Dr. Suzanne Brainard
Director
Women in Engineering
University of Washington
Loew Hall, FH-10
Seattle, WA 98195

Dr. Marjorie L. Budd
Chief
Policy and Curriculum Initiatives
Office of Personnel Management
1121 Vermont Avenue, NW, 1200
Washington, DC 20005

Dr. Linda Cain
Program Director
Science and Engineering
  Education Division, Box 117
Oak Ridge Assoc. Universities
Oak Ridge, TN 37831

Dr. Patricia Campbell
Campbell-Kibler Associates
Groton Ridge Heights
Groton, MA 01450

Dr. Burt H. Colvin
Director of Academic Affairs
National Institute for Standards
  and Technology (NIST)
Administration Building, A-521
Gaithersburg, MD 20899

Dr. Eugene H. Cota-Robles
Special Assistant to the Director
National Science Foundation
1800 G Street, NW, Room 428
Washington, DC 20550

Dr. Theodore J. Crovello
Dean
Graduate Studies and Research
California State University
714 Administration Building
5151 State University Drive
Los Angeles, CA 90032

Dr. Mary Frank Fox
Department of Sociology
213 Oswald Tower
University of Pennsylvania
University Park, PA 16802

Mr. Dan Frownfelter
Manager of Human Resources
Staffing Projects, Hughes Aircraft
P.O. Box 45066, MS/C128
Los Angeles, CA 90045-0066

Dr. Marilyn Gowing
Assistant Director
Research and Development
Office of Personnel Management
1900 E Street, NW
Washington, DC 20415

Dr. Margaret Graham
Manager of Research Operations
  and Organizational Learning
Xerox Palo Alto Research Ctr.
3333 Coyote Hill Drive
Palo Alto, CA 94304-1314

Dr. Marguerite Hays
ACOS for Research
VA Medical Center--MS 151
3801 Miranda Avenue
Palo Alto, CA 94304

Dr. Mario Jarvis
Manager
University Relations and Special
  Programs
AT&T Bell Laboratories
Crawfords Corner Road
P.O. Box 3030
Holmdel, NJ 07733-3030

Dr. Harriet H. Kagiwada
Sigma Delta Epsilon President
Graduate Women in Science
6446 East Lookout Lane
Anaheim, CA 92807

Dr. Jane Butler Kahle
Condit Professor of Science
  Education
418 McGuffey Hall
Miami University
Oxford, OH 45056

Dr. Margrete S. Klein
Program Director
National Science Foundation
1800 G Street NW--Room 1225
Washington, DC 20550

Dr. J. Scott Long
Indiana University
Ballantine Hall
Department of Sociology
Bloomington, IN 47405

Dr. Yvonne Maddox
Deputy Director
Biophysics and Physiological
  Sciences Program
NIGMS
National Institutes of Health
Westwood Building, Room 905
5333 Westbard Avenue
Bethesda, MD 20892

Dr. Ellen F. Mappen
Director
Douglass Project for Rutgers
  Women in Math, Science, and
  Engineering
P.O. Box 270
Douglass College
New Brunswick, NJ 08903-0270

Dr. Jacqueline P. McCaffrey
Director of Special Projects
College of Natural Sciences
W.C. Hogg 204
University of Texas
Austin, TX 78712

Dr. Sherri McGee
University Programs Manager
Office of Human Resources and
  Education
NASA Headquarters, Code FEU
Washington, DC 20546

Dr. Eve L. Menger
Director of Research
Corning Incorporated
Houghton Park, SP-FR-02=10
Corning, NY 14831

Dr. Maresi Nerad
Special Assistant to the Dean
  for Research on Graduate
  Education
4th Floor, Sproul Hall
University of California, Berkeley
Berkeley, CA 94720

Dr. Paula Rayman
Director
Women in Science Project
Center for Research on Women
Wellesley College
Wellesley, MA 02181

Dr. Leon M. Schwartz
Vice Chancellor for
  Administration (Emeritus)
University of California, Irvine
1401 Mariner's Drive
Newport Beach, CA 92660

Dr. Judson Sheridan
Vice Provost for Research and
  Dean of the Graduate School
University of Missouri
202 Jesse Hall
Columbia, MO 65211

Dr. L. Nan Snow
Executive Director
Graduate Fellowships for
  Minorities/Women in the
  Physical Sciences
University of California
Mail Code D-016
LaJolla, CA 92093

Dr. Elizabeth K. Stage
Director
NCSESA Critique & Concensus
National Research Council
2101 Constitution Avenue, NW,
HA 486
Washington, DC 20418

Dr. Ruth Ann Verell
Deputy Associate Director
University and Science Education
Office of Energy Research
 (ER-80)
1000 Independence Avenue SW
Washington, DC 20585

Dr. Harry Weiner
Program Officer
Alfred P. Sloan Foundation
630 Fifth Avenue
New York, NY 10111

Dr. Barbara Wilson
Group Head
Jet Propulsion Laboratory
4800 Oak Grove Drive
Pasadena, CA 91109

Dr. Linda S. Wilson
President
Radcliffe College
10 Garden Street
Cambridge, MA 02138

Dr. Lynn E. Wolfram
Branch Manager
BP Research Center
4440 Warrensville Center Road
Cleveland, OH 44128

OTHER PARTICIPANTS

Dr. Juana Vivo Acrivos
Professor of Chemistry
One Washington Square
San Jose State University
San Jose, CA 95192

Dr. Mary R. Anderson
Director, Graduate Career
 Change Program
Department of Industrial and
 Management Systems
 Engineering
Arizona State University
Tempe, AZ 85287-5906

Dr. Patricia A. Baisden
Deputy Division Leader
Chemistry and Materials Science
 Dept.
Lawrence Livermore National
 Labs
P.O. Box 808, Mail Stop L-310
Livermore, CA 94551

Dr. Joanne Rossi Becker
Professor of Math and Computer
 Science
San Jose State University
3192 Malvasia Ct.
Pleasanton, CA 94566

Mr. Robert M. Belknap
Staff Planning Associate
Shell Oil Company
One Shell Plaza
P.O. Box 2463
Houston, TX 77252

Dr. Lynn E. Bertuglia
Chair of the Women in
  Engineering Task Force
NSPE
P.O. Box 418769
Kansas City, MO 64141

Dr. Ann Boyd
Chair
Department of Biology
Hood College
Frederick, MD 21701

Dr. Peter Cannon
Managing Partner
VRE Company
2957 Seaview Avenue
Ventura, CA 93001

Dr. Francis P. Collea
Director
Research & Sponsored Programs
CSU, Office of Chancellor
400 Golden Shore
Long Beach, CA 90807

Dr. Nancy Cook
Washington M.E.S.A. State
  Coordinator
353 Loew FH-18
University of Washington
Scattle, WA 98195

Dr. Philip E. Coyle
Principal Labs Associate Director
Lawrence Livermore National
  Labs
P.O. Box 808, L-1
Livermore, CA 94550

Ms. Sheila D. David
Senior Staff Officer
Water Science and Technology
  Board
2101 Constitution Avenue, NW
HA 462
Washington, DC 20418

Dr. Cinda-Sue Davis
Director
Women in Science Program
University of Michigan
330 E. Liberty Street
Ann Arbor, MI 48104-2289

Ms. Catherine J. Didion
Executive Director
Association for Women In
  Science
1522 K Street, N.W., Suite 820
Washington, D.C. 20005

Ms. Claudia Dissel
Director
Corporate Council for
  Mathematics and Science
  Education
National Research Council
2101 Constitution Avenue, NW
HA 494
Washington, DC 20418

Dr. Arden Dougan
Chemist
Lawrence Livermore National
  Labs
P.O. Box 808
Livermore, CA 94550

Dr. Laurel L. Egenberger
Director of Operations
Quality Education for Minorities
1818 N Street, NW, Suite 350
Washington, DC 20009

Dr. Mary Ann Evans
Assistant to the Provost
Iowa State University
107 Beardshear Hall
Ames, Iowa 50011-2020

Dr. Rebecca Failor
Nuclear Chemist
Lawrence Livermore National
 Labs
P.O. Box 808, Mail Stop L-387
Livermore, CA 94551

Dr. Pamela Ebert Flattau
Director
OSEP, Studies and Surveys Unit
National Research Council
2101 Constitution Ave., GR-412
Washington, DC 20418

Dr. Elizabeth O'Connell-Ganges
Program Assistant
Douglass Project
P.O. Box 270
Douglass College
New Brunswick, NJ 08903-0270

Dr. Glenda Gentry
Research Associate
Electron Microscopy
Sandia National Labs
P.O. Box 969
Livermore, CA 94550

Dr. Deborah Gerber
Consultant
1149 Brioso Court
Vista, CA 92083

Dr. Angela B. Ginorio
Director
Northwest Center for Research
 on Women AJ-50
University of Washington
Seattle, WA 98195

Ms. Kathi Guiney
Employment Manager
Western Digital Corporation
8105 Irvine Center Drive
Irvine, CA 92718

Ms. Rae Ann U. Hallstrom
Senior Design Engineer
Babcock and Wilcox
P.O Box 351
Barberton, OH 44203-0351

Dr. Caroline L. Herzenberg
Physicist
Argonne National Labs
9700 South Cass Avenue
Argonne, IL 60439-4845

Dr. Carol Hollenshead
Director
Center for the Education of
 Women
University of Michigan
330 E. Liberty Street
Ann Arbor, MI 48104-2289

212

Dr. Elizabeth S. Ivey
Provost
Macalester College
1600 Grand Ave.
St. Paul, MN 55105

Dr. Gary D. Keller
Regents Professor
Hispanic Research Center
Arizona State University
Tempe, AZ 85287-2702

Ms. Susan C. Kemnitzer
Deputy Division Director
Engineering Infrastructure
  Development
National Science Foundation
1800 G Street, NW (1776G)
Washington, DC 20550

Dr. Marcia S. Kierscht
Dean
Graduate School and
  Professional Studies
Hood College
Frederick, MD 21701

Ms. Sharon Koons
Affirmative Action Rep.
Hewlett Packard
3000 Hanover Street
Palo Alto, CA 94304

Ms. Liisa Kuhn
Research Assistant
College of Engineering
University of California
Santa Barbara, CA 93106

Ms. Kelley R. Brandt-Lang
Senior Human Resources Analyst
Shell Oil Company
P.O. Box 2463
Houston, TX 77252

Dr. Barbara B. Lazarus
Associate Provost for Academic
  Projects
Carnegie Mellon University
Pittsburgh, PA 15213-3890

Ms. Renee S. Lerche
Manager
Ford Motor Company
Room 306
The American Road
Dearborn, MI 48121

Dr. Sharon Luck
Director of the Women in
  Engineering Program
101 Hammond Building
Penn State University
University Park, PA 16802

Dr. John F. Mateja
Faculty/Student Program Leader
Division of Educational
  Programs
Argonne National Labs
9700 South Cass Avenue
Argonne, IL 60439

Ms. Catherine Morrison
Vice President
Families and Work Institute
330 7th Avenue
New York, NY 10001

Dr. Carol B. Muller
Assistant Dean
Thayer School of Engineering
Dartmouth College
800 Cummings Hall
Hanover, NH 03755-8000

Dr. Indira Nair
Associate Department Head
Department of Engineering and
  Public Policy
Carnegie Mellon University
Pittsburgh, PA 15213

Dr. Cynthia Palmer
Chemist
Lawrence Livermore National
  Labs
P.O. Box 808, MS L-234
Livermore, CA 94550

Dr. Helen M. Ranney
Professor Emerita of Medicine
6229 La Jolla Mesa Drive
La Jolla, CA 92037

Dr. Karol Ruppenthal
Manager of the Employment
  Equity and Compliance Center
Lawrence Livermore National
  Labs
P.O. Box 808
Livermore, CA 94550

Dr. Kate Scantlebury
Professor
University of Maine
206 Shibles Hall
Orono, ME 04469

Dr. Neena B. Schwartz
William Deering Professor of
  Biological Sciences
Northwestern University
2153 Sheridan Road
2-120 Hogan Hall
Evanston, IL 60208-3520

Ms. Karen P. Scott
Education Outreach
  Coordinator
Sandia National Labs
Division 8526
P.O. Box 969
Livermore, CA 94550

Dr. Cecily Cannon Selby
Avon Products Director
  and NYU Science
  Education Professor
45 Sutton Place South
Apartment 17-I
New York, NY 10022

Dr. Rose M. Sergeant
Education Coordinator
Center for Particle Astrophysics
NSF Science and Technology
  Center
301 Le Conte Hall
University of California
Berkeley, CA 94720

Dr. Elaine Seymour
Director of Ethnography and
  Assessibility Research
Campus Box 580
University of Colorado
Boulder, CO 80309